ISBN 978-1-331-06377-3
PIBN 10140049

This book is a reproduction of an important historical work. Forgotten Books uses state-of-the-art technology to digitally reconstruct the work, preserving the original format whilst repairing imperfections present in the aged copy. In rare cases, an imperfection in the original, such as a blemish or missing page, may be replicated in our edition. We do, however, repair the vast majority of imperfections successfully; any imperfections that remain are intentionally left to preserve the state of such historical works.

1 MONTH OF
FREE
READING

at
www.ForgottenBooks.com

By purchasing this book you are eligible for one month membership to ForgottenBooks.com, giving you unlimited access to our entire collection of over 1,000,000 titles via our web site and mobile apps.

To claim your free month visit:
www.forgottenbooks.com/free140049

English
Français
Deutsche
Italiano
Español
Português

www.forgottenbooks.com

Mythology Photography **Fiction**
Fishing Christianity **Art** Cooking
Essays Buddhism Freemasonry
Medicine **Biology** Music **Ancient**
Egypt Evolution Carpentry Physics
Dance Geology **Mathematics** Fitness
Shakespeare **Folklore** Yoga Marketing
Confidence Immortality Biographies
Poetry **Psychology** Witchcraft
Electronics Chemistry History **Law**
Accounting **Philosophy** Anthropology
Alchemy Drama Quantum Mechanics
Atheism Sexual Health **Ancient History**
Entrepreneurship Languages Sport
Paleontology Needlework Islam
Metaphysics Investment Archaeology
Parenting Statistics Criminology
Motivational

A SHORT HISTORY

— OF —

ANNAPOLIS ROYAL

THE

PORT ROYAL OF THE FRENCH, FROM ITS SETTLEMENT IN 1604 TO THE WITHDRAWAL OF THE BRITISH TROOPS IN 1854.

BY

W. M. MacVICAR, A.M.,

Head Master Annapolis County Academy.

TORONTO:

THE COPP, CLARK COMPANY, LIMITED.

1897.

PREFACE.

ANNAPOLIS ROYAL is known to have been intimately connected with the stirring events of a period extending over nearly three hundred years ; but comparatively few, even of its own residents, are acquainted with its history. A few works are extant affording valuable information respecting the history of the province at large, with occasional reference to this section of the country. The majority of our people, however, seldom see these books, or, if they do see them, fail to gather the continuous history of the town from the disconnected paragraphs of a general treatise.

The need existing among ourselves of definite knowledge concerning the prominent place we hold in the history of the continent, would, of itself, explain the appearance of such a work. Aside from this, the stranger who visits us desires to have in portable form the information he seeks to obtain respecting a locality of such absorbing interest. The present work aims to afford, in small compass, a concise record of the establishment and growth of French Port Royal until its capture by the English, and of events since the British occupation, with especial reference to military proceedings. The restricted limits of the volume render it necessary to omit, with few exceptions, mention of events that have occurred within the last forty years, many of which would be well worthy of recall in the time to come, although at present matters of general knowledge. To make the work brief, much interesting matter is withheld, and I fear it will be found that, in places, clearness is sacrificed in order to attain brevity. It has been the author's endeavour to secure the latest and best authority, especially on points in dispute, and he hopes that he has escaped any glaring inconsistencies in the treatment of his theme.   The author's thanks are extended to General James Grant Wilson, D.C.L., President of the New York Historical Society ; Abner Goodell, Esq., A.M., compiler of the Province Laws of Mass. ; Dr. J. G. Bourinot, C.M.G., Dominion House of Commons ; G. W. T. Irvine, Esq., Provincial Education Office ; Mrs. I. E. Morton, Clementsport ; Rev. H. D. de Blois, William Roach, Esq., H. L. Rudolf, Esq., Annapolis, and others who by their generous assistance have aided in making this work more accurate and efficient.

ANNAPOLIS ROYAL, N.S.
   June 7th, 1897.

CONTENTS.

vii

the mountain side. The limpid wave washes a shore of surpassing richness, protected by the sheltering dyke. This is
the approach to Evangeline's Land, the home of story. This
is the proper entrance to the garden of the province, the apple
orchard of the world. Come in early June, when the richly-
laden air is redolent of perfume, when the fertile valley
throughout its entire length of one hundred miles, is coloured
with the bloom of apple, plum and cherry ; or, come again in
autumn, when boughs are bending to their mother earth,
heavy with magnificent clusters of fruitage, and deny who
can that this is a land of generous promise. Remain till
winter winds are cold, and frosts are keen ; then, witness the
splendour of our setting suns, as, merging into a thousand
glories, they sink with lingering twilight into the golden west,
and you will say that Italy can scarce surpass our skies.

The tourist will find much of interest on the shores of the
fair Basin of Annapolis. The rivers that empty into it are
well stocked with salmon and trout ; the Basin itself and the
bay beyond abound with sea-fish. The forests that stretch
away toward the interior are the home of moose and caribou,
partridge and woodcock are found in season. If he is fond
of boating, a hundred trim craft are at his disposal, with
unrivalled facilities for testing their qualities. The tide that
comes bursting in from the Bay of Fundy, with its forty feet
of rise, brings water pure and invigorating for a saline bath.
If he wishes to linger where nature has not yet been improved
out of recognition, he can find no more congenial resort than
among the villages of this quiet region.

At the extreme west of the sheet of water called The Basin,
on the right and near at hand as we pass through the Gap, lies
the trim town of Digby. This possesses many attractions as a
summer resort. The hot air is tempered by the sea breeze that
finds its way from the Bay of Fundy. In front and stretching

away in the dim distance lies the land-locked haven of Port Royal. Beautiful drives abound in the neighbourhood, and unsurpassed facilities for sea bathing. The trip from Digby up the Basin is delightful. The water is, in fact, an inland sea sixteen miles long, triangular in shape, narrowing from a width of six miles in the west to one half at the extreme east, where the Annapolis River enters it through a narrow channel. On the north runs the unbroken ridge of the North Mountain, with a narrow belt of level or gently sloping land along the shore at its foot. On the south the land is undulating, gradually rising into ridges known as the South Mountain, which, at a distance, runs parallel with the North, and continuing east forms the southern boundary of the well-known valleys of Annapolis and Cornwallis. Three miles above Digby, the southern hills are pierced by the Bear River, on whose banks, four miles inland, nestles the charming village of the same name. This region is famous for its cherries, and is the Mecca of many a pilgrim when that delicious fruit is in season. Five miles beyond, the Moose River is reached, at whose mouth lies the picturesque village of Clementsport, with the beautiful valley of Clements Vale. A mile or two further on, Goat Island stretches across the Basin, leaving a narrow channel on each side for our passage. This island separates the broader Basin proper from the narrow portion above, which may be termed the estuary of the Annapolis River. Fertile farms, with comfortable homesteads, lie along both shores as we have advanced. The main channel passes to the north of Goat Island and approaches very near the shore.

At this stage passengers will be eagerly on the watch to catch the first sight of the roofs of old Annapolis Royal, the former capital of Nova Scotia, with the green slopes of its dismantled fortifications ; for, we infer, the intelligent traveller has some knowledge of its history. Before the earliest English landed at Jamestown, in Virginia, the French had settled on the shores of Annapolis Basin; we are therefore in the vicinity of the earliest settlement made north of Florida. While here skirting the northern shore, and awaiting the first sight of the historic town, take a careful survey of the land opposite the island, where the strait is narrowest; for exactly on this spot did the hardy Frenchmen first pitch their tents in August, 1605. Here, protected from the fierce north winds by the sheltering mountain, they built their dwellings, surrounded them with a fortification, and amid many privations and much uncertainty, began the heroic work of laying the foundation of French dominion in America. The domicile of this people gave character to the history of the locality for one hundred and fifty years. This land of hill and dale attracts us not alone for its surpassing beauty, but for its thousand memories. A knowledge of its romantic history invests the seemingly ordinary object with a halo of interest.

Yonder, now, may be seen the clustering homes of Annapolis Royal; but the student of history sees more than houses. In imagination there lies the scene of a century and a half of bitter conflict. There is, first, the clearing among the scattered oaks on the peninsula, where the settlers sowed their seed, six miles away from their habitations: next, a few low dwellings; then, a fort with its waving Fleur-de-lis; again, the hostile approach, a hasty summoning for defence, the murderous strife, repeated through the years. Such is the story of the quiet old town that slumbers beneath its leafy shade.

The many see only the fleeting present, but the favoured few are permitted to catch glimpses of the life of long ago. Strange faces pass before the vision while sitting by the fireside in evening meditation. Figures in curious and antique garb move indistinct in the twilight. Shadowy visitors of proud and courtly mien pace our streets, mingle in our transactions and claim residence among us. They are the ghosts of the memorable past who refuse to leave their earthly haunts. Men may come and men may go, with all the bustling changes of civilization ; but these abide forever.

The town of Annapolis lies six miles above Goat Island on a narrow peninsula one mile long, formed by a small stream called Allen's Creek, running from the south, and a bend in the main river, which here, before narrowing to its issue into the Basin, makes a wide detour. Extensive intervale borders both rivers. At the angle formed by the creek and the main stream lie the fortifications, covering an area of fully thirty acres. These are in a fine state of preservation, still showing the original lines, and presenting a formidable appearance. This fort was built after plans drawn by Vauban, the great French engineer, and consists of four bastions with connecting curtains to form the main defence. Outside these walls lie three ravelins. The ditch is now altogether dry, but in the early part of the eighteenth century had running through its centre a wet ditch protected by a palisade. Above this rose the walls of bastion and curtain to the height of thirty feet, faced with timber hewn in adjacent forests. On the parapet above lay logs, secured by pins, ready to be set rolling down upon the heads of assailants. The embankments appear difficult of ascent even now, after a century's rains have beaten upon them. What must have been their appearance to the venturesome storming party that had succeeded in passing the defences of the ravelins and wet ditch, and at last were beneath them, ready for the final assault ? The quadrilateral within bastions and curtains at one time contained many large buildings, but all, with one exception, have disappeared. The antiquated structure with immense chimneys that occupies the eastern side of the square was, in former days, the residence of his Britannic Majesty's officers stationed at Annapolis Royal. A long building, constructed, like the officers' quarters, of brick with a covering of wood, stood on the south, at right angles to the quarters. This was destroyed by fire in 1831, to the consternation of the garrison and inhabitants, as the magazine in the immediate vicinity held at that time one hundred and fifty barrels of gunpowder. Another long building, with many peaks on its leaded roof, occupied the side next the river, but was removed in the first part of this century. A three storey brick building with hip roof, which was used as barracks for troops, stood on the west near the sally-port. This building, which appears in some prints of the fort, was torn down in 1853. In the northern bastion, next the town, stood the block-house, a structure of English oak, which commanded the bridge over the moat and the common approach. This was torn down in 1881, much to the chagrin of the town people. A few articles of furniture, or walking sticks, dear to the hearts of their possessors, are all that remain of its timbers. Near the gateway leading to the town stood a long, low range of buildings, used as gun sheds by the English. These were burned quite recently. In the ravelin that protects the west bastion are to be seen the remains of furnaces where shot were heated to be used against attacking ships, as well as the pits where they were stored. There are two wells, one within the curtain, the other in the south ravelin. The old French wharf is still visible (*vide* plan), and a little from it is the dilapidated structure of the " Queen's Wharf," the inner portion of which was built by English soldiers after Nicholson's capture, but was extended for commercial purposes in recent years.

The first fort on this spot was probably constructed by Sieur D'Aunay in the year 1643. This was enlarged and improved by his successors, Brouillan and Subercase. Hostile attacks on Port Royal number about a score, of which three occurred before the erection of works on this site. The present fort has suffered ten regular sieges and was three times captured, while, time and again, it has anxiously awaited the attack that threatened but never began. Its capture by Nicholson, in 1710, finally established British ascendency. In 1896, a grant of money was made by the Dominion Government to restore the masonry of these fortifications, which was rapidly falling into decay. Much was done in that year, and a promise is given of an additional grant the present year, 1897, sufficient to complete the restoration. The most extensive repairs were put upon the prison in the west bastion, which has now resumed somewhat of its original appearance. The brick work of the old sally-port was strengthened and freshly banked. The old magazine in the south bastion, built by Subercase, in 1708, of stone brought from France by Brouillan, in 1702, requires much yet to be done before it is in a satisfactory condition.

The old French town lay up river from the fort, on what are now St. George and St. Anthony streets, with scattered dwellings along the road leading to L'Equille, where, again, there must have been quite a settlement in the neighbourhood of their mills. In the early days of the colony, the scattered settlers probably met for worship with the soldiery within the fortifications. When their numbers increased, a separate chapel was demanded; but where it was located, or whether more than one were built remains in doubt, as our knowledge is dependent on fragmentary traditions. We gather from Murdoch's history that the people had no church at the time of March's attack, in 1707, but met in the house of M. de Villieu, which stood near the fort. After that building was burned, the inhabitants worshipped with the soldiers in the garrison chapel. Four years previously, Governor Brouillan had been taking active measures to erect a commodious church, towards which eight hundred livres were subscribed in Port Royal, while King Louis XIV. himself donated a sum equivalent to four hundred dollars. The unsettled state of affairs in the colony, owing to the war with Great Britain, prevented the construction of this building.   We are informed by Rev. Henry D. De Blois, in a very interesting article recently (1897) contributed to the Halifax press, that the parish church of St. Ann was erected, in 1708, through the instrumentality of a French priest named M. Dicrville, but was occupied by the British as a Protestant church, after the ratification of the Treaty of Utrecht, in 1713.   This church was erected on glebe lands originally granted by the French Government, and subsequently given by Queen Anne for the use of the Church of England.   It stood in the space between Church and Drury streets, facing St. George, very near the present railway platform.   As St. Ann was the tutelar guardian of the Indians, we are led to infer that they attended service in this chapel. If the British seized this and used it as a place of worship, it is possible that the French may have built another chapel, as there is a popular belief that an old French chapel occupied a site near the coal sheds by the Acadia pier.   We are told that English emigrants, arriving in Annapolis on Palm Sunday about the year 1725, were much impressed when they landed, to see a procession of French worshippers with green branches in their hands, wending their way from their chapel in the "Lower Town."   An Indian who died a few years ago, at a very advanced age, used to say that, when a boy, he saw the foundation of the old French church in the neighbourhood mentioned, and many years ago, a cross, which is supposed to have surmounted this chapel, was found in the bottom of a well near the present Roman Catholic church.

The burial place of the French is said to have been the ground now comprised in the Roman Catholic cemetery, or in the vicinity.   A few years ago, residents on the east side of Drury Street, opposite the railway station, discovered human remains while digging holes for setting fence posts.   Five bodies in all were found, reposing in regular order, and therefore indicating a general burial place. As some of these were enclosed in hollowed trunks of trees, they must mark an early date. There may have been a church at L'Equille, or services may have been held there in private dwellings, as tradition assigns a chapel to that locality and a burial place as well.

Outside the fort, the traces of French habitation are few. The dykes that line the river banks are standing memorials to their patient industry. The venerable willows in the hollows, and the gnarled trunks of ancient apple and cherry trees bear pathetic witness to the fondness of this people for the never to be forgotten fields of France. An old cellar will sometimes bring to view remains of household treasures, curiously shaped bottles, bricks of peculiar make, bits of iron, now and then a lock or other reminder of the homely pursuits of a simple people. Marvellous stories are told of pots of gold that have enriched some lucky finder, but these discoveries are rare. The professional money hunter, and we have him with us, has not been successful in his finds. There are other remains of a different kind, which give evidence of affairs not peaceful. Ancient arms, fragments of shell, cannon balls large and small, are frequently dug out of the ground at the present time, to remind us that the halcyon days of peace did not always prevail.

Before the days of the French, in the centuries behind us, a primitive people occupied these lands. Other eyes, we do not know in what distant age, had rested with lingering delight upon the varied beauties of this sylvan paradise and marked them for their own. Long years before a Cabot had sighted the coasts of our fair province, or even the hardy Vikings of the North had attempted their perilous ventures, the dusky children of the forest had pitched their wigwams by the banks of the rushing L'Equille. There, in Nature's own amphitheatre, shut in about by the encircling hills, they dwelt secure. The waters at their feet were alive with the choicest products of the sea. In the spring-time, the salmon, shad, and gaspereau crowded the narrow stream even as they do in our day. The vast forests were their hunting grounds, from which they returned richly laden with the spoils of the chase. The skins of moose, caribou, bear, lynx, beaver, otter, furnished them with necessary clothing, and contributed to the comfort and decoration of the wigwam. With their hooks of bone or shell, or with skilfully constructed weir, they gathered a harvest from the finny tribes of the broader deep, and loved to join in the exciting chase of porpoise, as do their descendants now. Feathered game was plentiful ; wild fowl gathered in incredible numbers along our shores in spring and autumn, many of which remained through the summer season. The child of nature luxuriated in his life of wild abandon, feasting in times of plenty, but, alas, too sadly oblivious of the future to make provision for the possible day of scarcity and want. A drive of two miles takes us to the haunts of these ancient arrow makers, whose dwellings clustered beneath the leafy bowers of the forest primeval. In a land of beautiful retreats few rival this. Here the ground is sown thick with implements and weapons of an age of stone, before the advent of the white man had taught the use of others more improved.

After the English came, the town was restricted to somewhat narrow limits, owing to the large amount of military property. The Government House stood on the site of the present lighthouse. The Duke of Kent, father of Queen Victoria, when in command of the forces in 1798, erected a building on this spot for the use of the officers of the garrison. This house was destroyed by fire in 1833, when a ball was in progress in town. The exercise ground for the troops extended from the present residence of Capt. Nickerson to that of Mr. F. Pickels. The White House Field, frequently mentioned in old records, lay between the Episcopal church and the railway crossing. The

Governor's garden embraced the ground between the church and St. Anthony Street. When the regular forces were withdrawn from Annapolis Royal, in 1854, these lands were sold, and have since been occupied by residences. About that time the guns that had been mounted on the parapets were removed and taken to Halifax. A few others that did duty at Digby Passage and on the Granville shore have been brought to Annapolis to be placed in position. The destructive fires from which the town has repeatedly suffered have swept away all the old dwellings. We know where one or two of comparatively recent date once stood. The home of Commissary Williams, father of the famous Sir Fenwick Williams, of Kars, occupied the site of the Union Bank. It was removed when the bank building was erected, and a part of it is still standing on St. Anthony Street. The Winniett House, the residence of Sheriff Winniett, stood beside the Williams' house, where Victoria Street now opens. Judge Haliburton, the originator of the well-known character "Sam Slick," resided in the house that stands beside the Clifton Hotel. The English buried their dead in the burial ground adjacent to the fort. The earliest date now decipherable is that of 1720 on a slate slab. Another of 1740 is beside it. They mark the resting place of the wives of a garrison officer. A romantic story associates the name of the great Duke of Wellington with one who sleeps in the old Annapolis cemetery. The drives in the neighbourhood are charming and full of interest as well. Six miles down on the Granville side lay the old French and Scotch forts, and on both sides of the river sharp fighting occurred on the occasion of the Colonial invasions of 1704, 1707 and 1710.

Crossing Allen's Creek by the bridge, the old French road along the Basin is reached. This extended two miles up the creek to the site of their grist mill, crossed the narrow stream by the Three Bridges, turned to the left under the hill, and, following the course of what is now called Lovers' Lane, joined the present road near the L'Equille school house. This road may have had another outlet near the blacksmith shop. In the neighbourhood of this road, by the Lovers' Lane, are remains of earthworks thrown up by the French for the protection of their mill. Under these D'Aunay's ships sought shelter in 1643. There was also a continuation of the road on the western bank, past the grist mill, as far up as the present General's Bridge, where the river was crossed and the road built towards Port Royal through the sequestered settlement of L'Equille.

If escape is sought from the scorching heat of a summer sun, an excursion over the North Mountain to catch the cool breezes of the Bay of Fundy, or a visit to the secluded ice mines, hidden away in a deep gorge of the Granville hills, will prove refreshing. There is no lack of variety in the enjoyment to be had by the intelligent sojourner amid such scenes, and while he lingers under the shades of what a recent writer terms the "sleepy and moss-covered town" of Annapolis Royal, he may not be unwilling to listen to a recital of its romantic story.

SAMUEL CHAMPLAIN.

The first European to ascend the Annapolis river, June 17, 1604; erected the first dwelling at Port Royal, August, 1605; Founded Quebec, 1608.

CHAPTER II.

FOUNDING OF PORT ROYAL—VICISSITUDES—DESTROYED BY ARGALL.

1604-1613.

The story opens on the sixteenth day of June, 1604. That morning a small sloop had left St. Mary's Bay on a voyage of exploration. She entered the Basin of Annapolis in the afternoon. Upon her deck stood a few of the noblest sons of Old France, who had braved many dangers in search of fame, fortune, or a quiet home. The leader of the company was Pierre du Guast, Sieur De Monts, Governor of Pons, as well as an officer in the Royal household. He had come to America as King's Lieutenant in La Cadie, an undefined territory stretching from Belle Isle to the Chesapeake. His charter gave him ample powers to colonize new lands, with the exclusive right of trade in furs and other merchandise. Having left his ship and colonists in St. Mary's Bay, he was now in search of a place for settlement. With him was Samuel Champlain, a young man destined to win immortal honour, as the founder of French dominion in Quebec. He had borne an active part in the great Civil Wars in France, and, subsequently, had received a pension from his King for valuable service among the Spaniards in West Indies and Mexico. King Henry IV. had permitted him to accompany De Monts, on condition that he should prepare, for Royal inspection, a faithful report of his discoveries, with charts and maps. Beside them, gazing with kindling eye upon the beautiful picture, was Jean de Biencourt, Baron de Poutrincourt, who, after honourable service near his Sovereign, wished to bring his family to a quieter home in Acadia. Our voyagers admired the wide expanse of land-locked water and gave it the name of Port Royal. The next day, June seventeenth, they proceeded up the river for more than twenty miles, giving it the name Rivière de l'Equille, subsequently Dauphin, now Annapolis. The beautiful stretches of intervale satisfied the longings of Poutrincourt, who was weary of the pageantry of war and court. He resolved to make it his home. De Monts gave him a grant of the lands of Port Royal, confirmed subsequently by the King on condition of bringing colonists to cultivate the soil.

It is evident that Port Royal was satisfactory, as a place for permanent settlement, to neither De Monts nor Champlain. It did not offer facilities for the fur trade which De Monts had in view, while the absence of metallic ore detracted from its value in the eyes of Champlain. Acquainted, by his two years of West Indian life, with the great mines of Mexico and Peru, he was burning with strong desire to lay at his Sovereign's feet similar treasures. Quickly resuming their voyage, they skirted the shores of the Bay of Fundy, entered St. John Harbour, and finally fixed upon an island at the mouth of the River St. Croix as the seat of their colony. Poutrincourt returned to France in August, with the intention of settling Port Royal in the following summer.

The colony at St. Croix suffered untold misery during a winter of unexpected severity, losing thirty-five of their number by death. After unsatisfactory exploration as far south as Cape Cod, they decided to remove temporarily to Port Royal, where they would be sheltered from the piercing north winds, that had dealt so cruelly with them the previous winter. The place selected for settlement was a spot on the north side of the river, directly opposite Goat Island. The exact situation may now be determined, though no vestige of the construction remains to-day. The waters have encroached in part, while successive generations of plowmen have obliterated all traces of habitation. Champlain, in his journal, tells why the present site of Annapolis was not chosen. He says: "The whole country is filled with thick forests, except at a point a league and a half up the river, where there are some scattered oaks and many wild vines, which one could easily remove and put the soil under cultivation. We had almost resolved to build there, but thought it too far up the harbour."

Had Poutrincourt been permitted to return, he would doubtless have chosen that location, for on his arrival the following year, he had it cleared and planted. Having chosen a site, they constructed huts for dwellings, arranged in the form of a quadrangle, with an open court, while, with true French versatility, they at once began to lay out gardens and ornamental grounds. At the angles of the quadrangle nearest the water, two rectangular platforms were constructed, protected by palisades. On these cannon were mounted. Champlain built himself a summer house above their fort, where he had a fish pond, and also cut a road to a trout brook some distance below, now called Shafner's brook. De Monts went to Europe in the autumn, promising to send supplies in the spring. Forty-five men were thus left to spend the first winter in the little settlement at Port Royal. In their hastily constructed dwellings, built of green timber, lacking any semblance of drainage, they were destined to fight a stern battle against disease and cold. Pontgravé, their leader, worked energetically to alleviate their distress, but, in spite of all his efforts, twelve of his men died. At his request, the Indians brought furs and a supply of fresh meat, but, with savage dislike for steady manual labour, they refused to assist in the arduous work of grinding the corn.

On the return of spring, Pontgravé and Champlain endeavoured to find a place further to the south for the colony, but, after many delays, had the misfortune to wreck their craft on

2

the rocks at Digby Gap. The sloop which was built to repair
this loss, and launched June, 1606, was probably the first vessel
built in what is now the Dominion of Canada. The season
wore on, but no ship came with the expected supplies. Hope
died out as their stores ran low, for, owing to the uncertainty
of their movements, no seed had been sown in the spring.
With heavy hearts they prepared to leave Port Royal, in
hopes of falling in with some of their countrymen near
Canseau. Two brave fellows, Taille and Miquelot, agreed to
remain in charge of the fort until relieved the succeeding year.
The party sailed on July seventeenth. On the twenty-
seventh, the two men in the fort saw to their delight a ship
enter the Basin, from whose peak floated the ensign of France.
They gave her a salute of four guns, to which she made reply.
This ship was the *Jonas*, seventy-one days out from Rochelle,
with men and supplies for Port Royal. On board were De
Monts and our old friend Poutrincourt, who had nobly come
to the aid of De Monts, when he saw the difficulties his friend
was experiencing in obtaining support. Accompanying Poutrincourt was Marc Lescarbot, a clever lawyer of Paris, who
afterwards wrote a history of the colony. Pontgravé and
Champlain, providentially detained in St. Mary's Bay by an
accident, learned of the arrival of the *Jonas*, and returned to
Port Royal. Poutrincourt, to whom this place had been
granted in 1604, wished to make Port Royal his permanent
residence, and at once began cultivation of the soil. The spot
he selected for a clearing was a league and a half up the river,
where "we had thought," says Champlain, "to make our
abode"; the very fields on which the town of Annapolis now
stands. Although the season was advanced, wheat, rye, hemp
and other seeds were sown. At the end of August, the *Jonas*,
with De Monts on board, sailed for France, while Poutrincourt
and Champlain remained to explore the coasts and establish
the habitation on a permanent basis. Lescarbot, who com-

manded the fort in their absence on a voyage of exploration as far as Cape Cod, proved himself to be an efficient leader. He surrounded the fort with a ditch, to render it dry and comfortable, had the carpenters at work fitting the buildings, and made charcoal for the forge, which was kept active fashioning tools for the workmen. When the explorers returned, this genial Frenchman prepared a grand reception in their honour, displaying the coats-of-arms of the two leaders wreathed with evergreen.

In order to break the monotony of existence during the lonely winter, Champlain contrived what he called L'Ordre de bon Temps. The fifteen gentlemen who sat at the table of Poutrincourt, the Governor, took turns in performing the duties of steward for a single day. The Grand Master, for the time, laid forest and sea under contribution, and the table was constantly furnished with delicate game and choice fish. At each meal, a ceremony becoming to the dignity of the order was strictly observed. At a given signal, the whole company marched into the dining hall, the Grand Master at the head, with the napkin over his shoulders, his staff of office in his hand, and the glittering collar of the order about his neck, while the other members bore, each, in his hand, a dish loaded and smoking with some part of the delicious repast. At the close of the day, when the last meal had been served and grace had been said, the master formally completed his official duty by placing the collar of the order upon the neck of his successor, at the same time presenting to him a cup of wine, which the two drank to each other's health and happiness. The Indians, young and old, crowded round to witness the ceremony so strange in their eyes. Their old chief, Membertou, used often to take his seat at the table of the Governor. This warrior had been present on the landing of Cartier at Gaspé, in 1534. Timber was cut that winter for building two small vessels, whose seams were filled with the

gum of fir trees, in the absence of pitch. A corn mill was also
built at the head of tide water on Allen's Creek. On Champlain's map, the mill stood on the left bank of the stream, a
hundred yards below the present well-known Three Bridges.
The first road in Acadia was begun from the fort at Goat
Island to Digby Gap.

As soon as spring opened, the work of getting in the seed
was vigorously prosecuted. But, on the twenty-fourth of May,
1607, in the midst of their busy activity, a sloop arrived bearing orders from De Monts, for Poutrincourt to remove the
colony at once to Canseau, where the *Jonas* lay ready to
carry them to France. All their fondest hopes were dashed
at a blow. Things at home had gone wrong with De Monts.
When he returned to France in the autumn of 1606, he found
a powerful combination of merchants working to secure a
removal of his monopoly, which, it was alleged, was proving
destructive to French commerce ; while his clerical foes
charged him with neglecting the spiritual interests of the
Indians. In consequence of these representations the King
had revoked his charter. The order for departure was
obeyed, but Poutrincourt himself lingered a few weeks until
the grain in the fields had ripened. Membertou was left in
charge of the fort and mill with all their grain, a trust he
faithfully fulfilled. It was the desire of Poutrincourt to take
with him to the French King specimens of the rich products
of Acadia, for he entertained the hope of establishing his
family in Port Royal, despite the removal of De Monts'
suzerainty. Having gathered his treasures, he joined his
companions at Canseau and returned to France. He so won
the heart of King Henry IV. that the grant of Port Royal
given him by De Monts was confirmed by the Monarch.

We must now bid adieu to our heroic friends De Monts,
Champlain and Pontgravé. Their names are written in

the ancient encampment is a charming spot in the midst of an amphitheatre of encircling hills, through which a brawling stream pours itself into quiet tidal waters. At the very door of the wigwam the canoe rested lightly. Aside from early associations, the place affords, in picturesqueness óf situation, a striking example of sylvan beauty. In all Nova Scotia it would be difficult to find a spot appealing more strongly to the romantic imagination. In this neighbourhood have been gathered, in recent years, many fine specimens of primitive weapons, fashioned with exquisite skill. In one locality we find a spot where the ."ancient. arrow-maker wrought." We note the infinite patience with which he pursued his task, the ceaseless endeavour after repeated failure ; for a score of disappointments is at hand to emphasize his one success.

Biencourt, son of Poutrincourt, a youth of nineteen, was sent to France to carry to the King the news of the conversion of the natives and to obtain supplies for the ensuing winter. On his arrival, France was in commotion on account of the assassination of King Henry IV., and Biencourt found it beyond his power to obtain in season the needful provisions. The youthful voyager having surmounted the obstacles that delayed him, with bravery approaching hardihood attempted an Atlantic passage on a little ship of sixty tons, in the month of January, 1611. He reached Port Royal after long delays, bringing with him two Jesuit missionaries, Fathers Biard and Masse, who had been sent to the colony at the expense of the Queen-mother, Mary de Medici.

The death of Henry IV., who had been his personal friend, made it necessary for Poutrincourt himself to return to France in the interests of the colony. He left Port Royal in July, 1611, having appointed his son Biencourt to the command of the little colony, which now consisted of twenty-two persons. At this time, the charter rights of De Monts over the lands of La Cadie were transferred to Madame de Guercheville, wife of the Governor of Paris, a woman filled with zeal to establish a religious society in the New World. After protracted disputes between her supporters and the friends of Poutrincourt, whose special rights in Port Royal did not please this lady, an expedition started in 1613 under Saussaye, consisting of thirty persons. Sailing to Port Royal, they took on board the two Jesuit fathers and proceeded to the coast of Maine, where they formed a settlement near Mount Desert. They there came into collision with the English, who claimed all that part of North America on the strength of Cabot's discovery. An armed force from Jamestown, in Virginia, under Capt. Samuel Argall, broke up the colony in the summer of 1613 and sent most of its members to France. Soon after, Argall found his way to Port Royal, piloted, some say, by the Jesuit father Biard. On his arrival he found no person to defend the fort, as all the men were at work in the fields five miles away. He at once set fire to the fort, which was consumed with all its dwellings and stores. He even defaced with a pick the arms of France, and the names of De Monts and his associates, which were engraved on a stone within the enclosure. The poor fellows up river were powerless, but, fortunately for them, the English were unaware of the existence of the mill and barns. Biencourt had an interview with Argall for the purpose of arranging terms of trade or a division of territory, but all his proposals were haughtily rejected. The continent of North America was not large enough to satisfy the grasping avarice of this brutal marauder. The French, who had expended large sums in the colony, were left completely destitute. Many found their way elsewhere, but it seems certain that, in spite of the destruction of their dwellings and defences, many settlers lingered in the neighbourhood. Williamson tells us that Biencourt was still resident at

Port Royal, in 1617, with a small French colony.   In 1619, missionaries were appointed to minister to the needs of those French who still remained at Port Royal.   Poutrincourt is said to have returned the next year, 1614; but, when he saw the blackened ruins of his habitations, all his bright hopes of establishing a colony in Acadia died out.   He alone had been the warm advocate of a settlement at Port Royal ; and, as he thought that the English had been induced to attack it by his opponents, the Jesuits, he abandoned further efforts, returned to France and entered the service of the king, where he met his death at the siege of Mèry-sur-Seine, in 1615.

CHAPTER III.

FORT ST. LOUIS—SCOTCH IN NOVA SCOTIA.

1613-1632.

When Argall destroyed Port Royal, England and France were at peace; but no protest seems to have been made by the latter country, whose court was at the time too much absorbed in party intrigue to seek redress for the wrongs of an impoverished noble in the far away forests of America. The story of Port Royal for a few years after Argall's capture is obscure and somewhat contradictory in its details. It seems certain that the mill on Allen's Creek still stood, and that any dwellings or barns in the vicinity of the cultivated land on the point, now Annapolis Royal, were not disturbed. The Indian encampment was in the immediate vicinity of the mill; and while the homeless French sought refuge among their dusky friends, it is quite reasonable to suppose that they did not neglect the tillage of the soil. They well knew that the natives were reduced to great straits for want of food in previous winters, and steps to secure a supply of grain and vegetables would be taken by leaders so experienced as Biencourt and La Tour. It is also probable that, at this time, individual Frenchmen selected sites for abodes convenient to the cleared land and the rich marshes near at hand. Some of the settlers, however, found their way to Europe; some wandered north to the shores of the St. Lawrence, where Champlain was bending his great energies to the establishment of a Royal Colony of France. Others, again, were coming to take the place of those leaving the shores of Acadia. Adventurous Frenchmen were led to choose a life of freedom in a country where the inhabitants were friendly and trade promised profitable returns. In 1619, a French trading company established a post at the St. John, for the purpose of carrying on a trade in furs with the Indians, easily reached by the waters of that great river.

Among the French living at Port Royal, in 1613, was Claude La Tour, a Huguenot of noble family, who had lost his fortune in the Civil Wars in France, and had come to Acadia accompanied by his son Charles, then a boy of fourteen. After Argall's visit, the elder La Tour established a trading post at the mouth of the River Penobscot, a place closely associated with the history of Port Royal. His son, Charles, remained to share the fortunes of his leader Biencourt, the young vice-admiral. The semi-savage nature of their life, spent in intimacy with the Micmacs, led them at times to other localities. While residing near Cape Sable they built a fort of logs and earth, to which they gave the name Fort St. Louis.

On Biencourt's death in 1623, or on his departure from Acadia in 1621, as recently discovered documents throw some doubt on the commonly accepted story of his death in Acadia, Charles La Tour was named as his successor, and heir to his property at Fort St. Louis and Port Royal. This remarkable man, whose career forms so notable a chapter in Acadian history, married, at Port Royal, a young French lady of noble and exalted character. Shortly after assuming control in the colony, La Tour removed, with a number of followers, to Fort St. Louis, which he proceeded to strengthen and fortify as his headquarters. On the outbreak of hostilities between England and France, in 1627, his father, Claude, who had been driven from the Penobscot by the English, in 1626, was sent to France with a message to the King. In this communication, La Tour asked the King for a supply of arms and ammunition to put his defences in proper shape. He stated

that the Indians were faithful and his French supporters re-
liable. The King, in response to his request, sent out a fleet
of eighteen ships with one hundred and thirty-five pieces of
ordnance, and stores of ammunition sufficient to put Port
Royal and Quebec in an efficient state of defence. As this
fleet neared the shores of Acadia, in 1628, it was captured by
an English force under Sir David Kirk. The elder La Tour,
who was returning with the fleet, was sent as a prisoner to
England. Kirk next sailed to Port Royal, and left men to
prepare for a colony of Scotch settlers, who arrived the same
year under a son of Sir William Alexander and established
themselves on the Granville shore. Kirk was one of a company formed in Scotland to trade and colonize in a territory
named Nova Scotia, comprising the present provinces of Nova
Scotia and New Brunswick. Sir William Alexander, pro-
moter of this enterprise, had received a grant in 1621, confirmed in 1625 by Charles First, as King of Scotland. An
Order of Knights, called "Baronets of Nova Scotia," was
instituted to further the interests of the company and provide
funds.

On the formation of the company, an attempt had been
made to bring out a number of Scotch emigrants. These
passed the winter 1622-1623 on Newfoundland, and the next
summer sailed along the coast of Nova Scotia nearly to Cape
Sable, but returned to England when they learned that the
lands of Port Royal were occupied by the French. In his
endeavours to destroy the colonies of France in America,
Kirk had overlooked Fort St. Louis, near Cape Sable, at that
time the rendezvous of all the unsettled French in Acadia,
under the leadership of Charles La Tour. Here this resolute
man, supported by his hardy countrymen and the Micmac
tribes assembled in his vicinity, awaited events. His father,
Claude, had been taken a prisoner to England, but was soon
released from his bonds and received at Court. He was

induced by the solicitations of the many Huguenot refugees then in London to change his allegiance, and, together with his son Charles, was created a Baronet of Nova Scotia, with a grant of territory along the coast from Yarmouth to Lunenburg. In return for this concession, the elder La Tour was to plaht a Scotch colony at Port Royal, and obtain possession of Fort St. Louis for the King of Great Britain. He left Britain, in 1630, with a number of colonists on board two vessels thoroughly equipped and provisioned. On communicating with his son at Fort St. Louis, Charles indignantly rejected the overtures made by the British. He replied, that he held his fort in obedience to his liege sovereign, the King of France, and was prepared to defend it against all comers. His father's entreaties and threats failing to move the stubborn son, the British assaulted the works on two successive days, but were driven back with loss. As the commanding officer would not allow his men to be sacrificed in further fighting, the elder La Tour was compelled to proceed with the colonists to the Scotch settlement at Port Royal. On arriving at Port Royal a fort was erected on the site of the previous French fortifications. This work was of a more enduring character than the constructions of the French, for traces of the lines have continued nearly to the present. There are old men living to-day, 1897, who remember, as boys, playing on the ramparts of the Old Scotch Fort, so called. These Scotch settlers had bitter trials from the start. Thirty of their number died the first winter, and the survivors seem to have lingered on with no definite aim. The French settlers on the St. John, at Fort St. Louis, and in the outlying districts, were no doubt bitterly hostile, while the great body of Indians lost no opportunity to harass those who were the foes of their firm friends and allies. The presence of La Tour among the Scotch, alone saved them from hostile attack.

The capture of Quebec by Kirk, after peace had been declared in 1629, stirred the French authorities to look more closely to their interests in America. In 1630, two ships were sent out from Bordeaux with men and arms for La Tour at Fort St. Louis, which he was to use as best suited his purpose. He at once opened correspondence with his father at Port Royal, and induced him to desert his Scotch companions and come to him, on representation that England was soon to give up her claims to Nova Scotia. After careful deliberation, the two La Tours and the French commander, Marot, determined to build a strong fort at the mouth of the River St. John, where there was a powerful tribe of Indians to assist them against their English enemies. The site was advantageous too, for their expected trade in furs. The younger La Tour remained at Fort St. Louis to hold it against an expected attack from the Scotch. The King of France—in recognition of the important work done by Charles La Tour—appointed him the King's Lieutenant-General in Acadia. The original commission, recently found, is now in possession of the Colonial Society of Massachusetts. The Company of New France made the king's commission effective by sending out a plentiful supply of stores and arms to the faithful and zealous La Tour. In the meantime, before work had progressed to any extent on the St. John, Charles I. of England, who had married a French princess, was preparing to surrender to France the lands which he had granted to one of his own subjects, and on which large sums had been expended. On the twenty-ninth of March, 1631, Acadia was restored to France by the Treaty of St. Germain-en-Laye.

CHAPTER IV.

THE TWO RIVALS, LA TOUR AND D'AUNAY.

1632-1653.

The Company of New France, a rich and powerful association formed in 1627 by the great minister, Cardinal Richelieu, now began energetic measures of colonization. Isaac de Razilly, a relative of the cardinal and captain in the French navy, was sent out with two armed ships carrying colonists and stores. He bore commission from the King of France, authorizing him to remove the Scotch from Port Royal, as well as letters patent from Charles, as King of Scotland, ordering his subjects to yield to the demands of Razilly without resistance. Sir Wm. Alexander wrote, as well, to Captain Forrester, the commander of the Scotch, asking him to deliver the place to De Razilly. On board the ship was Charles de Menou, seigneur d'Aunay de Charnisay, who subsequently played so important a part in the history of Port Royal.

The Scotch had suffered so terribly in their short residence that a change was welcome, though it included the surrender of their fort. Some of their number chose to remain with the French, married in the country, and finally became merged in the French population. De Razilly having carried out the commands of his superiors and received the submission of the Scotch, left Port Royal and planted a colony at the mouth of the river La Have, where a fort of the usual character was erected. We have no clear account of the state in which Port Royal was left, or of its people ; but, no doubt, there were at this time residents on permanent holdings who were not disposed to change their domicile at the whim of each succeeding leader. The fields that had been cleared, the rich grass lands near by, the fact of dwellings already built and the vicinity of the Indian encampment, with the existence of a corn mill, all point to such a conclusion.

While Port Royal was thus enjoying a period of quiet obscurity, events were transpiring elsewhere that had an important bearing upon her subsequent history. It is necessary to remind our readers that England had not been idle in planting colonies in these early years of the century. All along the coast from Virginia to Machias, settlements were made, the most important of which were in the neighbourhood of Boston. These took alarm when the King of England so unceremoniously handed over Port Royal to another nation, and with good reason ; since the French claimed that the territory surrendered, extended south to the Delaware, and included the English colonies of Plymouth and Massachusetts Bay. The French, acting on this claim, drove away the English from Machias and from Penobscot, in which place they built a fortified trading post, under command of D'Aunay, a relative of Razilly. When the colony of Massachusetts Bay heard of De Razilly's proceedings, they began hastily to protect themselves by works at Nantasket, and took possession of Agawam, now Ipswich, for fear that so fertile a district might be occupied by the troublesome French. Although the colonies of New England were the national and commercial rivals of their neighbours in Acadia, they did not scruple to trade with them for mutual profit, even when such intercourse was interdicted by the authorities. It is interesting to note the intimate relationship which existed between the two colonies. Indeed, the story of both for the following one hundred years, is a recital of bitter and seemingly implacable feuds arising from their mutual rivalries and animosities.

3

After a few years of neglect, Pòrt Royal was granted, in 1634, to Claude, the brother of Isaac De Razilly. In 1635, Charles La Tour received an allotment of lands at the mouth of the River St. John, as lieutenant for the king in New France.   The fort begun by his father was now put in a strong state of defence.   On the death of Isaac De Razilly, in 1636, his brother, Claude, handed over his rights in Acadia to D'Aunay, who was then at Penobscot.   This man possessed a bold and enterprising spirit.   He was ambitious to undertake an extensive trade with the natives, and engage in other enterprises requiring a large force of employees.   To supply the necessary provisions for his numerous followers, he required a strong agricultural colony at some central station.   Port Royal was splendidly adapted to his purpose.   It had rich soil and a fine harbour.   He took prompt measures to remove the colonists from La Have, giving them farms on the shores of the Basin and along the banks of the beautiful river, which winds for forty miles through wide stretches of level intervale. These lands won the hearts of the exiles whose youth had been passed amid just such fields in sunny France.   They knew how to raise the protecting dykes that would convert these low stretches into rich harvest fields.   D'Aunay, in addition, brought out from France twenty families, and Port Royal was at last established as the permanent emporium of trade and commerce in Acadia.   But D'Aunay, lieutenant for the king, and possessor of Port Royal and Penobscot, could not rest content while another lieutenant held important posts in these fair fields.   His grasping disposition led him to seek all the profits, though the field was large enough for both, and though his rival was in possession of privileges richly deserved on account of faithful and arduous service.

The history of Port Royal for the ten years, 1635-1645, is an account of the bitter strife between D'Aunay and La Tour.   Each had his headquarters in the territory of the

other ; for Maine and New Brunswick were D'Aunay's territory, while Acadia, with the exception of La Have and Port
Royal, belonged to La Tour. D'Aunay had influence at
court; his father was a king's counsellor and a strong advocate of his son's cause. It is not surprising, then, considering
the character of Cardinal Richelieu, and the Huguenot connec-
tions of La Tour, that orders were issued by the king, in 1641,
commanding La Tour to embark for France immediately,
to answer charges made against him. D'Aunay had directions
to use force, if necessary, to compel La Tour, and take possession of his fort and property. A king's ship was sent out to
bring the accused home for trial, but La Tour refused to obey
the command, on the ground that the king's orders were
based on misrepresentation. D'Aunay was afraid to attack
the stronghold of his rival, and repaired to France, where we
find him, in 1642, borrowing large sums of money from
Emmanuel La Borgne to expend in waging hostilities against
his fellow-countryman. La Tour, knowing the efforts that
were being made by his enemy, sought assistance from the
New England colonists and from his Huguenot friends in
Rochelle, who sent out a force of one hundred and forty
men in an armed ship called the *Clement*.

In the spring of 1643, D'Aunay fitted out a force at Port
Royal of five hundred men, which sailed in two ships, a
galliot, and several small craft to the attack of La Tour's
fort across the bay. While his fort was invested by this
formidable force the *Clement* arrived off the harbour unknown
to the besiegers. La Tour, leaving the charge of the fort
to his heroic wife, succeeded in getting on board the relieving
ship and sailed with all haste to Boston, where he was permitted to hire a force of one hundred and fifty men, who
embarked on four ships. D'Aunay, patiently blockading the
fort, and expecting an early surrender, was greatly surprised
when the five ships from Boston came in sight. He did not

await attack, but sailed in haste for Port Royal, and took his
vessels up the little river called Allen's Creek, until they
grounded near the mill, which his men, we are informed, proceeded to fortify. The captain of the New England force, who
was not hired to wage offensive warfare, at first tried, without
success, to effect a reconciliation between the two rival Frenchmen, with both of whom his colony was on friendly terms.
The colonial captain then permitted as many of his men as
wished to accompany La Tour in his attack on the mill,
which was captured and burned after a stubborn resistance.
In this engagement three of D'Aunay's men were killed and
one taken prisoner, while La Tour had three men wounded.
The New Englanders accompanied La Tour to the St.
John, where they captured a pinnace freighted with a rich
cargo of furs belonging to D'Aunay. Taking their share of
these, they sailed away home, where they arrived in August,
1643, after an absence of thirty-seven days. The success of
La Tour led D'Aunay to take more serious precautions for
the safety of his colony. He determined to construct a
stronger fort in the best possible position, to protect his infant
colony of scattered agriculturists, and prevent his new mill
from suffering a like destruction. The site chosen was the
present position of the Annapolis Royal fortifications, admir-
ably situated to command both the main river on which their
farms lay, and the Allen's Creek, up which the mill was built.

Historians assume that Charnisay's previous fort was on the
site of that of Champlain, where the Scotch had been located.
If there had been a fort at the narrows, opposite Goat Island,
it is difficult to understand why D'Aunay, with his vessels,
did not seek protection under its bastions, instead of proceed-
ing a distance of seven miles further, two of which were up
the sinuous waters of a narrow stream. It seems scarcely
reasonable to suppose that he would have sailed straight past
his fort to run his ships aground in an unprotected place. It

is fair to assume that he placed his ships under the guns of his defences, and we may look for these defences in the vicinity of the old mill on Allen's Creek. In fact, there is to-day distinctly visible along the crest of the hill overlooking the mill, and commanding the creek approaching it, a rampart of earth extending for a long distance. This rampart was evidently raised to defend the approaches to the mill. If we consider the circumstances on D'Aunay's arrival, the conclusion we have reached seems the more probable. The French about Port Royal when he came, in 1636, would be on the cleared lands near the mill, and in the neighbourhood of the richest pasturage. The fort of Champlain was surrounded by dense woods, near the mountain foot, where there was little chance for agriculture. Both he and Poutrincourt went up the river five miles to plant their grain, and ground it at the mill, two miles further away. Would D'Aunay, the clear-headed and prompt man of affairs, repeat such a folly when he arrived with his colony of farmers? He would naturally allot the very best lands to his settlers, and these lands would comprise the beautiful alluvial levels in the immediate vicinity of Annapolis Royal. The grist mill was of paramount importance to such a community, and it is not strange to find him raising fortifications to defend it. The narrative of La Tour's attack is consistent with the theory that D'Aunay's only fort was a position guarding the approach to the mill, and within a few hundred yards of it.

When his new fort was well under way, D'Aunay again crossed the Atlantic to secure aid in his further efforts against La Tour. Lady La Tour was in France, at the same time, strengthening her husband's interests. D'Aunay attempted to have her arrested, but she escaped to England, and, after many delays, reached the St. John, by way of Boston, with supplies for her husband. After D'Aunay's return, negotiations were opened with the Massachusetts colony, to secure its neutrality in the quarrel between him and La Tour. In October, 1644, an agreement was entered into binding Port Royal and Massachusetts Bay to keep firm peace with each other. This agreement prevented the English from giving open aid to La Tour, but did not prevent them from trading with him, and furnishing supplies, of which he stood much in need. A vessel in this trade was captured by D'Aunay, in defiance of the treaty, and her crew put upon Partridge Island, in the winter time, without fire, and under wretched shelter. When Governor Endicott protested, D'Aunay replied in high tone, demanding satisfaction for the loss of his mill at the hands of the New Englanders, in 1643.

The reckless quarrel between the rival Frenchmen continued, until both men had exhausted their resources and completely impoverished themselves. La Tour had mortgaged his lands to parties in Boston, while D'Aunay had borrowed immense sums from La Borgne, whose presence in Acadia we shall soon have to note. In February, 1645, D'Aunay attacked the fort at St. John, when La Tour was absent and the garrison small, but the devoted wife inspired her garrison with her own courage, manned the walls, and beat off the besiegers. In April, while La Tour was still absent, a final attempt was made upon the place. Through the treachery of a sentry, an entrance was gained by the besiegers ; but the defenders, with Lady La Tour at their head, fought with such spirit that the assailants were driven back with heavy loss. Finally, Lady La Tour agreed to surrender if the lives of her brave companions were spared. This was assented to and the gates opened. D'Aunay basely broke his word of honour, and hanged every man of the garrison but one, who was compelled to be executioner of his comrades ; while the devoted and courageous woman, whose lofty heroism had often animated their flagging energies, was forced to witness the barbarous massacre. These dreadful scenes broke her heart.

Three weeks from the day of the capture, she breathed her last, and was laid to rest by the banks of the stately river.

D'Aunay had now attained the summit of his hopes. He had establishments at Port Royal, on the St. John, and at Penobscot, and controlled the trade of a territory half as large as France. He required three hundred men to defend his forts. At Port Royal, where he established his headquarters, he built mills for grinding corn and sawing timber, and began the system of dykes by which the extensive salt marshes have been reclaimed. He was the owner of two large farms at Port Royal, and engaged quite extensively in ship building, as we read of two vessels of seventy tons, five pinnaces, and several shallops built by him during his stay. These were probably constructed on the banks of Allen's Creek, near the mill, where a shipyard existed in recent times. He also erected a church and established a school for the instruction of children.

On his visiting France, in 1645, the King ordered a vessel to be equipped to bring him to Acadia, when he returned loaded with princely favours. A long dispute ensued between the Massachusetts colony and D'Aunay over the destruction of his mill, in 1643. The French at first claimed eight thousand pounds damages, but at last accepted the gift of an elegant Sedan chair from Governor Winthrop, in lieu of money compensation. D'Aunay did not live long to enjoy his triumph. We have no particulars of his death, save that he was drowned at Port Royal, in 1650. No regrets are expressed for the sudden death of the man, who, with the power to overcome enemies, lacked the ability to make friends.

La Tour, who had passed the years after 1645 among the French and Indians of Quebec, repaired to France, when he learned of D'Aunay's death. He succeeded in clearing himself of the charges made against him, and returned to America with larger powers than he ever before possessed. The long-standing enmity between the two families had a romantic ending in the marriage, at Port Royal, of La Tour with the widow of his former rival. This took place on the twenty-fourth of February, 1653. La Tour continued to reside at the River St. John, with trading posts at Penobscot and Cape Sable, while Port Royal was held by La Verdure on behalf of the children of the deceased D'Aunay.

CHAPTER V.

PORT ROYAL THE FOOTBALL OF THE NATIONS—CAPTURES BY THE
ENGLISH—RESTORATIONS TO THE FRENCH.

1653-1701.

Emmanuel La Borgne, the creditor of D'Aunay, obtained judgment in the courts for two hundred and sixty thousand livres, and came to Acadia armed with authority to take possession of his estates. He made his headquarters at Port Royal while he matured a scheme to obtain control of all Acadia. La Verdure continued in charge of the fort as commander for the King. Among other hostile acts, La Borgne seized Nicholas Denys, the historian, who was exercising his fishing rights in Cape Breton, and imprisoned him in the dungeon at Port Royal. He was planning the capture of La Tour's fort on the St. John, when the appearance of a strong hostile armament in the Basin filled him with consternation. Although there was peace between England and France, a fleet of four ships, on board of which were five hundred men, under command of Major Robert Sedgewick of Charlestown, and Captain John Leverett, of Boston, had been sent to dispossess their somewhat troublesome French neighbours. This force, at first prepared against the Dutch at Manhattan, was directed against Acadia with the reported consent of Cromwell. Penobscot and the St. John had been visited before the fleet appeared at Port Royal.

La Borgne refused to surrender, and opposed the English, who landed three hundred men on the south side of the Basin. When the sergeant in charge of the French was killed, his force retreated in disorder to the fort. Within his defences,

La Borgne had one hundred and fifty men and abundance of military stores, while an armed ship lay moored near by. He had not the courage, however, to make more than a show of resistance, and surrendered on fair terms, August seventh, 1654. La Verdure obtained favourable consideration for ·the children of D'Aunay, who had much property at Port Royal. The inhabitants were permitted to retain their lands, and enjoy their own forms of religion. Captain John Leverett was left in command of the fort until the arrival of Colonel Temple, an English officer sent out by Cromwell in 1657. La Tour, who had been permitted by the English Government to hold his lands, sold out to Temple, and retired to spend the evening of life in the enjoyment of his hard won fortune. He died in 1666.

Temple had his headquarters at Penobscot, but kept a garrison at Port Royal, and at a point up the St. John called Jemseg. He expended large sums of money in disputes with rival claimants, owing to the vacillating conduct of the King, Charles the Second. The French were demanding the restoration of Acadia, during the lifetime of Cromwell, but never received satisfactory replies. On Cromwell's death, their importunity increased. At last, after the short war ending in 1667, Charles agreed to restore the country to France, in exchange for one half the little Island of St. Christopher, in the West Indies. Delays occurred, but, in the year 1670, the Chevalier de Grand-fontaine arrived in America, with commission from the monarchs of France and England to receive possession of Acadia. Temple obeyed the order of his King, and yielded possession on the second of September, 1670. He at once laid claim against the Government of England for damages, but no requital was ever made. Grand-fontaine established himself at Penobscot, as we are informed the fortifications at Port Royal had crumbled away. We infer from this that D'Aunay's later fort, which La Borgne surrendered to Major Sedgewick, was probably nothing stronger than the palisaded structure of an earlier period. La Borgne's son, Alexander, who had taken the title Belleisle, took up his residence at Port Royal about 1667, and assumed rights of proprietorship as seigneur, in which we find him coming into conflict with Grand-fontaine's authority.

A census of Port Royal was held in 1671, when we find a total of sixty-eight families, aggregating three hundred and sixty-one people. In addition to agriculturists, there was a priest, one surgeon, a weaver, four coopers, a farrier, two armorers, a mason and a maker of edge tools. Many of the family names are familiar to our ears to-day : Comeau, Doucet, Gaudet, Landry, Robichaud, Melanson, Petipas, Terriau and Thibaudeau. Three hundred and sixty-four acres of land were under cultivation, and upwards of one thousand domestic animals owned. These people had occupied the easily worked lands along the river, until these grew to be a scarcity. But they had heard of the wonderful reaches of Chignecto and Mines, visited long before by Poutrincourt, Biencourt and Father Biard, and adventurous spirits were ready to plant colonies of Port Royal in these far-away fields. Jacob Bourgeois and Pierre Arsenault took settlers to Chignecto about this time. Shortly after, Pierre Theriot, Claude Landry, Antoine Landry and René Le Blanc were associated in forming a colony at Mines. This settlement became a favourite residence, and soon grew to be the richest and most populous district in Acadia.

The years succeeding 1670 were quiet ones at Port Royal, save for the occasional disputes with Belleisle. Arrivals from France were adding to the population, so that by 1680 quite a village was formed. Successive governors had made their headquarters at Penobscot, or on the St. John, until the year 1684, when M. Perrot, Governor of Montreal, was appointed to the command in Acadia. He selected Port Royal for his residence, where he proceeded to billet his force of thirty soldiers among the inhabitants, owing to the bad condition of the fort. A request was made to the home government for fifty more soldiers, besides guns, and military stores, and for means to construct a palisaded fort to enclose the Governor's house, men's quarters, and storehouses. A corvette was also asked for to suppress buccaneers of all nationalities, who had made these coasts their prey, having in 1684 captured six fishing craft belonging to Port Royal.

The census of 1686 showed an increase in the settlement of two hundred and thirty-one, besides the garrison. Many of the names were new, showing increase by immigration. Belleisle and D'Entremont, who had married daughters of Charles La Tour, owned extensive tracts of land in the vicinity. Perrot was succeeded, in 1687, by M. de Menneval. The instructions to this governor give evidence that Louis the Fourteenth was showing a deep interest in the welfare of the colony. He was ordered to stop unlawful trade, prevent licentiousness, and maintain religious services. The resources of the country were to be studied, and attention given to agriculture. Thirty men were added to the garrison, and four thousand livres, with tools and materials, were sent out for rebuilding the fort. This was no longer to be built of timber, but especial orders were given to construct it of earth, with fascines and turf, while great care was to be exercised in guarding the arms and ammunition. De Menneval, like his predecessor, Perrot, was too much bent upon self-aggrandizement to enter fully into the spirit of these instructions, in consequence of which work progressed so slowly, that the outbreak of war between England and France, in 1689, found them all unprepared for defence. The officials at Port Royal, Governor, Judge and Procureur du Roi, seem to have passed their time in mutual recrimination, accusing one another and each excusing himself. Letters to France were filled with personalities of the most trivial nature. All seemed to think their highest duty lay in the line of personal profit.

As we said, war broke out in 1689. William of Orange sat upon the throne of England, and hastened to use his newly-acquired power against his enemy, Louis the Fourteenth. The years that followed were filled with carnage and massacre among the early settlers in America. Frontenac, the able administrator of Canada, hurled his forces of regulars, rangers and savages against the defenceless villagers of New England, and aroused every colonist to acts of bitter retaliation. The people of New England at once made preparations to attack Port Royal. An expedition, fitted out in Boston, sailed on the ninth of May, 1690, under the command of Sir William Phipps. It consisted of seven vessels, one of which was a frigate of forty guns, carrying in all a force of seven hundred men. On the approach of the enemy, the picket of three men on guard at the entrance to the Basin, discharged a mortar to give the alarm, and started in a canoe for the fort, which was reached near midnight. Menneval at once discharged a cannon to summon the settlers, many of whom lived at long distances, but only a few responded. Affairs were in a desperate state. The walls were unfinished ; of his eighteen cannon, not one was in position, while his garrison of seventy men were destitute of officers. Preparations were being made to retire up river with all their stores, as far as Round Hill, where they hoped to make a successful defence. A brig was being loaded for that purpose ; but at the urgent solicitations of two priests, Fathers Petit and Trouvé, Menneval consented to treat with the enemy.—It is worthy of note, that a short time after this, a memorial was presented to the French Government, proposing to abandon the fortifications at Port Royal, and construct a fort of timber six miles up river, at Round Hill, capable of lodging one hundred men, and mounting four twelve-pounders, four eight-pounders, and four four-pounders.—When a summons came to surrender, the messenger was detained and Petit sent to treat with Phipps. The clever priest, assuming a defiant air, secured favourable terms. The garrison were to be carried to France, with arms and baggage. The inhabitants were not to be deprived of their lands, the church was to be spared and the people permitted to worship unmolested. Port Royal then surrendered; but Phipps made a pretext to break these terms when he saw that the shrewd priest had over-reached him. He claimed that the conduct of some French soldiers, in breaking into a store after the surrender, had violated the treaty. The English proceeded to strip the church, broke into the priest's house, plundered private property, even to the Governor's purse, and took Menneval himself, with most of his followers, to Boston, where they were thrown into prison.

Before his departure, Phipps summoned the French settlers and made them take the oath of allegiance to the Crown of England. Instead of leaving an English force to maintain order, Phipps chose a number of the Acadians to form a Council, with a French sergeant named Chevalier as President, who swore to administer affairs under the English flag and the government of Massachusetts. They then sailed away, carrying a large amount of plunder which had been taken from the fort and warehouses of the town. One trading company alone met with losses amounting to fifty thousand crowns. Some time after the withdrawal of Phipps, the Massachusetts authorities sent over Colonel Eward Tyng to assume command as Governor of Port Royal. With him was John Nelson, a nephew and heir of Sir Thomas Temple. Both had the misfortune to fall into the hands of the French, so that no English-speaking representative was to be found at Port Royal.

A few days after Phipps had left, a ship arrived direct from France, loaded with stores of every description for the military at Port Royal. She brought recruits for the garrison, and two officers of high rank. These were Villebon, brother of Menneval, who had come out to lead the Indians of Maine, and Saccardie, an accomplished engineer, whose mission was to place the fort in thorough repair. Villebon, aware that English ships were in the vicinity, determined to proceed at once to the River St. John and fortify the old site at Jemseg. There, for the next few years, operations were planned against the colonists of New England by the French and their Indian allies.

After Villebon's departure to make fortifications at Jemseg, and before the ship-load of stores had sailed for the St. John, a sad disaster befell Port Royal. Two piratical craft, hearing of the defenceless condition of the post, entered the Basin, and after burning sixteen houses on the Granville shore, sailed up river. Here they burned twelve more near the village, in one of which was a mother with her children. After committing terrible ravages, hanging two of the inhabitants and looting the whole settlement, they sailed away, taking with them the ship with its load of stores, on board of which was Saccardie, the engineer, and the former Governor, Perrot.

In 1691, Villebon visited Port Royal, hauled down the English flag, and, in the presence of the willing Acadians, took formal possession in the name of the King of France. The people of Massachusetts had not attempted the difficult task of maintaining communication with Port Royal, across a water infested with free-booters, and scoured by the French cruisers. A French writer of the period describes Port Royal as "no more than a paltry town, somewhat enlarged after 1689, by the accession of inhabitants who had left the French shores of Maine owing to the war. In fine, Port Royal is only a handful of houses two stories high, and has but few inhabitants of any note. It subsists upon the traffic of the skins which the savages bring hither to truck for European goods." While Villebon, from Jemseg or Nashwaak, was harassing the English with forays, or defending his position against attack, Port Royal was quietly recruiting her strength. The mills had not been destroyed,—thanks to their secluded position—as we read that, in 1696, plank was sawed at Port Royal for the French on the St. John, while provisions were bountifully supplied, both by the settlers at Port Royal and those at Mines or Grand Pré. Although the regulars had been withdrawn, the people had organized six companies of militia, armed with such weapons as were at hand. M. de Falaise was sent in 1697 to command these, but was relieved the next year by M. Batiste.

When England and France made peace in 1697, by the Treaty of Ryswick, the French were permitted to retain their possessions in Acadia. France again manifested an interest in Port Royal, which had been neglected for years. An officer sent out to report upon the condition of affairs, recommended the abandonment of the River St. John on account of its poor harbour, and the re-establishment of headquarters at Port Royal. The French Government decided to follow the advice of its delegate, and issued orders to Villebon accordingly. He reluctantly abandoned the enterprise of rebuilding Fort La Tour, at the mouth of the St. John, and proceeded with his accustomed energy to construct works at Port Royal that would require a garrison of four hundred men. Belleisle and D'Entremont were at this time granting fishing privileges to English vessels, while Villebon was endeavouring to keep them off the coast altogether. Villebon died in 1700. He was succeeded by M. de Brouillan, Governor of Newfoundland, who came across country from Chebucto (Halifax) by way of the flourishing settlement of Grand Pré. The people of this district promised to cut a road that year, 1701, for thirty miles towards Port Royal, to open easier communication between the two places.

Brouillan, who was a man of ardent temperament, approaching rashness, took steps at once to make Port Royal the actual headquarters. Fort La Tour was razed to the ground, and its guns and buildings removed across the bay, where the works were taking shape in something like their present form. The people were assembled and reprimanded for their neglect in providing timber, and were ordered to furnish sufficient to construct palisades around the entire works. Brouillan, however, was ambitious to have a fort of stone, and made recommendation to that effect, as well as for the construction of a redoubt at Digby Passage. Port Royal, after many vicissitudes, was again a garrison town, and the residence of a governor. Its defences were receiving some attention at the hands of the new chief, but much remained still to be done. The town itself was the general trading centre for the whole country. Villebon wrote that the people were well supplied with food, and had a surplus for sale. Many spars were sent to France; wool was good, and most of the people were dressed in their own homespun; fruits, pulse and garden stuff were excellent; provisions were cheap—beef two cents a pound; a pair of chickens ten cents; eggs, five cents a dozen; cattle, six to eight dollars each;—a statement which gives us a realization of the condition of affairs in old Port Royal, the opening year of the eighteenth century.

CHAPTER VI.

EXPEDITIONS OF CHURCH, MARCH AND WAINRIGHT AGAINST PORT
ROYAL.

1701-1707.

The peace that followed the Treaty of Ryswick was not of
long duration. It was broken by the great war of the Spanish
Succession, a war associated with the victories of Marlborough,
in Europe, but pursued with relentless cruelty as well in the
forest glades of America, where, as before, the Indians fought
on the side of the French. From Maine to Connecticut,
the inhabitants lived in a frenzy of fear from the terrible
attacks of an insidious foe, whom Vaudreuil, the Governor-
General of New France, urged on and provided with necessary
equipment. The English colonists at first attempted reprisals.
Rewards were given for the scalps of the enemy ; but little or
no impression could be made upon these children of the
forest, who retired to inaccessible swamps or wooded hills.

The authorities then adopted a scheme advocated by Colonel Benjamin Church. This was to retaliate upon the French
settlements in Acadia, as the best means of protecting their
own homes from invasion. Steps were accordingly taken, in
1704, to equip an expedition for that purpose. The French
at Port Royal were, as usual, unprepared on the outbreak of
hostilities. Brouillan seems to have worked in a leisurely
way on the earthwork, while maturing his scheme for con-
structing a more pretentious fort of stone. The war, however,
hastened operations ; all thought of stone was laid aside,
and every possible effort made to push on the work of construction. A force of men from Grand Pré came to assist

the small garrison in this labour. Even with their assistance the task was an onerous one. When we look at the massive heaps of earth remaining to-day, after the leveling agency of two centuries has been at work, we are filled with admiration at the audacious courage of the man, who, with a force of one hundred soldiers and a small working party of the inhabitants, attempted such a construction. It was estimated that it would take the two years, 1703 and 1704, to complete it. Although the French Government contributed liberally toward this work, Brouillan was at times compelled to issue paper money to meet his bills. It was at his earnest request that stone for the construction of buildings was brought from France, on account of the exceeding hardness of the material in the neighbourhood.

In addition to work on the fort, he built and furnished a hospital, and warmly seconded the efforts of the inhabitants to secure a new place of worship. Eight hundred livres were contributed by the inhabitants for this object, to which King Louis himself—growing devout in his declining years—added one hundred pistoles ($400). The Governor was appointed honorary warden, in recognition of the warm interest he manifested. Brouillan had to contend against the opposition of dissatisfied subordinates, who were constantly sending complaints home to France. He was accused of gaining possession of Hog Island by unfair means, of ruling with great harshness, even to the infliction of torture upon his soldiers, and of excessive charges in collecting fees. Des Goutins, the judge, Labat, the engineer, and others are concerned in these disputes, which seem to have arisen from jealously, common to life in a station so isolated as Port Royal.

The force which the English colonists were raising gathered at Boston in May, 1704. The command was given to Colonel

Ben Church, who had taken an active part in the previous war. It consisted of five hundred and fifty men, with a fleet of fourteen transports and three war vessels. Leaving the armed vessels in the Basin at Port Royal, Church proceeded up the bay to the unprotected settlements of Grand Pré and Chignecto, where he burned the dwellings, destroyed the crops, killed the cattle, and tore down the dykes to injure the grass lands. His ships rejoined their consorts at Port Royal Basin in July, 1704, and came to anchor near Goat Island. Some men were landed, a few settlers taken prisoners, but no decided attempt made to attack the place. After a few days of seeming indecision, a council of war was held, and the assault abandoned on account of the activity and numbers of the French, and the insubordination of his own troops. The men were embarked, anchors weighed, and the fleet sailed away, to the great relief of Brouillan. Port Royal had been spared the devastation inflicted upon her children at Chignecto and Grand Pré. Opinion in Massachusetts charged the leader with cowardice, but the General Assembly voted him thanks for good services to Queen and Country.

At the time of Church's visit work was progressing on the fort, but difficulties were experienced owing to the sandy nature of the soil. Six hundred feet of the ramparts were washed down by the spring rains shortly after this, and the engineer was charged, as a matter of course, with faulty construction. The fascines were not properly placed, it was said. The defenders were no better than their embankments. The officers were young and inexperienced, and the recruits of no account whatever. A ship of forty guns was asked for to oppose an enemy's landing. In 1705, Brouillan went home to France, on account of ill health, leaving Bonaventure, a captain in the Royal Navy, in command of the fortress. The troops then numbered one hundred and eighty-five men, who were brought into a state of health and efficiency by the intelligent methods of this capable officer. The fort, however, in the year 1705, remained unfinished, despite the efforts of Labat. Port Royal, in these years, was the rendezvous for the privateers that were hovering about the coasts of New England ready to pounce upon a hapless fisherman or trader. The prisoners were brought here for safe keeping, until exchanged for the Frenchmen in like situation among the English. When the exchanges were effected, the agents of the two countries were said to make other exchanges to their mutual advantage. Indeed, during these hostilities, and previously, trade with the English colonies was secretly carried on, as prices in Boston were much lower than at Port Royal, and the French gladly purchased goods when they could do so without the knowledge of their officials. Some of the latter, too, were accused of being parties to this illicit intercourse, and to have largely profited by it. Vessels had been built at Port Royal from time to time, but were often of small size. In 1705, however, a large ship was built to serve the purpose of a frigate, for the defence of the coasts of the Bay of Fundy. She was launched on December the first of that year, and named *La Biche*—" The Hind."

De Brouillan, on returning to Acadia, died on board ship near Chebucto Bay. His body was buried at sea, but his heart was preserved and buried on October third, 1705, with suitable honours, near the cross in the vicinity of the proposed church. Next year, 1706, M. de Subercase, a man of great ability and amiable manners, arrived at Port Royal as Governor of Acadia. Bonaventure, though disappointed in thus losing his position of chief command, loyally assisted Subercase, and, for the first time in twenty years, something like harmony reigned in the colony. It is pleasing to note

the personal friendliness existing between the Governors of
Massachusetts Bay and Port Royal. Soon after the arrival
of Subercase at Port Royal from Placentia, he sent M. du
Forillon to Boston with a force of thirty-five prisoners, whom
he was to exchange for a like number of French. He was
detained for some time, while these latter were being got
ready, but finally was sent back to Port Royal with his
countrymen, and bearing besides, as a gift from the genial
Governor Dudley of Massachusetts, to Governor Subercase
at Port Royal, nothing less than a hogshead of wine and four
barrels of beer. These martial heroes did not forget the
amenities of life amid the dire necessities of war.

Whatever policy lay in this gift, it is known that before Du
Forillon left Boston, Governor Dudley opened correspondence
with Governor Winthrop of Connecticut, and Governor Cranston of Rhode Island, proposing an expedition of one thousand
men against Port Royal. Winthrop, though he admitted Port
Royal to be the Dunkirk of America, did not acquiesce in the
proposal. Cranston joined heartily in the project, and measures were at once taken to equip the force. Colonel March,
of Newburg, was chosen leader, with Colonels Wainwright
and Appleton of Ipswich in command of the regiment of the
red, and Colonels Hilton of Exeter, and Wanton of Newport,
in command of the regiment of the blue. In the first we find
companies from Ipswich, Newburg, Boston, Lynn and Salem,
etc., in the second from Exeter, Newport, Reading, Taunton
and Charlestown. An officer of the Royal Engineers, Colonel
Redknap, had charge of ordnance and siege operations, with
third seat at the Council Board, while Captain Stacley, of Her
Majesty's ship *Deptford*, fifty guns, was to rank next the
commander-in-chief.

The ill success of the whole expedition seems, in great part,
owing to the jealousies that arose between the Colonial

officers on the one side, and the British commanders, who took little pains to conceal their disdain for their companions in arms. Captain Southack, in the *Province* galley of twenty-four guns, who had sailed with Church in 1704, assisted the *Deptford* in convoying the fleet, while two or three of the numerous transports carried ordnance. This fleet, carrying over one thousand men, sailed from Nantasket on twenty-fourth May, arrived off Digby Gap on June sixth, 1707, and entered the Basin with so little delay, that the men on guard at the entrance scarcely had time to reach the fort before the ships were coming to anchor above Goat Island. The French were taken by surprise, but the calm courage of their leader restored their confidence. As soon as Subercase saw the hostile fleet, messengers were sent to notify the inhabitants, many of whom lived at a considerable distance. As these people were all enrolled in the militia, they were sent, on arrival, to oppose the advance of the enemy on both banks of the river.

The English in the meantime had landed far down the river, near Goat Island, and were slowly making their way through the woods. Colonel Appleton, with three hundred and twenty men from the Lynn, Salem, Taunton and Weymouth companies, and a number of Indians, got on shore on the north side shortly after four p.m., and did not pitch camp till nine; while the remainder of the troops, under March himself, were landed at five on the south shore. Colonel Appleton's force was attacked the next morning in a ravine, but succeeded in driving the French before them, with loss of two men only, and, at noon, reached a spot opposite the fort, where they fixed their camp. The French militia retreated to their boats, crossed the river and sought the shelter of the fort. The troops under Colonel March seem to have advanced up the Basin and along Allen's Creek without serious opposition, until they attempted to cross at the Three Bridges, where the French had prepared an ambuscade. The fight was then waged with intense vigour ; Subercase himself leading his own men, and having his horse shot under him. At last he was compelled to retreat, followed up the hill by the English, who advanced in the face of a brisk fire, with trumpets sounding, drums beating, and flags flying, and giving three huzzas as they charged the enemy. It is probable that the earthwork along the bank of the creek was used by the French in this defence. The English force pushed on, and pitched camp at the foot of the hill, now called Bailey Hill, in sight of the fort, to which the French retired in some confusion.

The Colonials were now encamped within a mile of the fort on the peninsula, and less than half a mile across the river ; but their difficulties were only to begin. Before them lay the prize for which they had made extensive preparation, but it was guarded by five hundred men, while on the ramparts and ravelin were mounted over forty guns—twelve, eighteen, twenty-four, and thirty-six pounders, the latter, however, pointing seaward. To take so formidable a place by assault was too hazardous an enterprise for the undisciplined militia of New England. Accordingly, it was thought best to reduce the place by regular siege. Soon, however, the lack of concert among the leaders showed itself. Redknap failed to bring his heavy guns into position against the defences, while Stucley, in his English man-of-war, lay far out of range. The Colonials made energetic efforts to capture the fortifications, but, without the support of their artillery, these were futile. In advancing against the works from the south, the English gained the cover of several buildings which stood near the fort on that side ; but Subercase at once had these destroyed.

For many days, the English contented themselves with making excursions to burn the dwellings and destroy the property of the inhabitants, but, on the night of the sixteenth, a determined assault was made upon the fortifications. The English began by a heavy fire of musketry, under cover of which five hundred men rushed to attack the breaches, which, from common rumor, they expected to find in a far worse state than they actually were. The defenders stood firmly by their guns, until the New Englanders, finding the fire too heavy for them, retired to the shelter of their approaches. In the early morning they left the vicinity of the fort, and, in accordance with the decision of a council of war to abandon the attack, were at once embarked. In this action the English claim to have burned the great magazine, church (Villieu's house, used for holding church service), and many houses near the north bastion of the fort, and to have fired from positions gained by them on the ramparts, into the buildings within the fort. The success of the defence was largely due to the timely arrival of sixty Canadians, who reached Port Royal about twelve hours before the fleet anchored. De la Ronde and Baron Castine rendered efficient service in attacking the English on the march.

Colonel March hesitated to return to Boston, where news of the capture of Port Royal was impatiently awaited. He caused the fleet to rendezvous in Casco Bay, from which place he wrote to Governor Dudley, attributing his failure to the lack of harmony existing among his officers, and to the fear of the men that they were to be left in Port Royal permanently as a garrison. In a letter from Commissary Arthur Jeffries to (it is supposed) Cotton Mather, written thirteenth of June, 1701, the blame of the result is laid upon the ship captains and Colonel Redknap, who, even after he had marked out a place on shore for posting his batteries, and had broken ground, threw up the undertaking with the excuse, that he could not risk his reputation in the hands of such officers as he had to support him. The delegation of three that carried letters from Casco to Boston met with a tumultuous reception. A mob of women and children, bearing wooden swords, met them at Scarlet's wharf with the cry of "Port Royal," "Port Royal," and thrust their swords at them, shouting, "Fie! for shame!" "Pull off those iron spits by your sides, for wooden ones are all the fashion now!"

Dudley at once took energetic measures to wipe out the disgrace of a repulse so ignominious. At the suggestion of Governor Cranston, of Rhode Island, three commissioners were appointed to supervise the conduct of the expedition, which was expected to renew the attack as quickly as possible. These were Colonels Hutchinson and Townsend, and John Leverett, Esq. The fleet was ordered to remain in Casco Bay, and the men forbidden to leave ship under penalty of death. In spite of this decree, however, deserters were so numerous that in two months, when the fleet was provisioned and ready for sea, the forces numbered only seven hundred and forty-three men. March, who was broken in spirit and in health, resigned his command after the fleet left Casco Bay, and Wainwright was appointed to succeed him. The expedition entered the Basin at ten o'clock on the morning of Sunday, twenty-first August, and came to anchor early in the afternoon. Subercase was not taken so completely by surprise this time, as notice had been given him that the English were preparing to renew their attack. Two English prizes, loaded with flour, hams, lard and butter, contributed a supply of wholesome food to his garrison, whose numbers were increased by the providential arrival of a French frigate under Bonaventure. Governor Dudley's instructions urged the English to land on the south side of the Basin, and reach the rear of the fort by way of Allen's Creek, but Subercase took advantage of their delay in landing to throw up defences on that shore. The troops were accordingly disembarked, Monday, in an orchard on the Granville shore, about two miles below the fort, and at once marched, under cover of the woods, to a point about one mile above the fort, where they took possession of some unoccupied houses.

Details of the events that followed are sadly contradictory. Charlevois has been the accepted authority up to the present, but the publication of Province Laws of Massachusetts, 1895, compiled by Abner Goodell, Esq., of Salem, differs with him in many respects. The English were prevented from crossing at the narrows, where they encamped, by the fire from the fort, and tradition says, as well by works which the French threw up on Hog Island itself. When the English attempted to throw up earthworks opposite the fort for mounting siege guns and mortars, they were forced to desist by a vigorous discharge of cannon and musketry. After remaining but one day at the narrows, the English retired to the landing place in the orchard, where they entrenched a camp, still within reach of the heavy guns on the sea walls of Port Royal. On the twenty-fourth, musketry firing was going on all day across river, between the English on the north bank and a large party of Indians on the shore at the fort. About four in the morning, while parties of the New England men were engaged in cutting brush, nine of them were cut off and killed by a large force of French and Indians who had crossed the river some miles above and had been lying in ambush. On the twenty-sixth, Colonel Wainwright writes a communication from "Port Royal Narrows," from the tenor of which, it is inferred, he is leading a force to cut the dykes and destroy the property of the settlers.

On the twenty-seventh, the English were compelled to abandon their entrenched camp and retire to a position three and a half miles down river, out of reach of the shells from the fort, and under protection of the guns of the ships. During the next few days, the militiamen of New England, crowded together in camp, without proper covering, lying on the bare ground, and provided with few of the necessaries of a campaign, grew sick and despondent. It was unsafe for small parties to leave their quarters, as the lurking Indians were ever ready to fall upon them ; at the same time their outposts were exposed to the galling fire of ambushed Frenchmen. The French account informs us that the English landed on the south side of the Basin on the last day of August, covered by the guns of the fleet, and advanced to attack the French, who were hidden in the woods. A desperate encounter ensued with varying fortune. Subercase himself left the fort in charge of Bonaventure, and hastened to the support of Castine and La Boularderie, who were bravely leading their compatriots. The English seem to have driven their opponents to the woods, and then hastened to their boats and embarked with speed. This fighting would have taken place on the shore at Upper Clements, but no mention is made of it in the Massachusetts records. The fleet dropped down stream on September first, and sailed away on the fourth from the scene of such lamentable discomfiture.

The inefficiency of Wainwright, the lack of spirit and determination among officers and men, with the smallness of the force, doomed this second attempt, a failure, at the outset. Had the subordinates shown a tithe of the zeal manifested by Governor Dudley, the result might have been different. Dudley lamented the supineness of Stucley in neglecting to engage the fort, or, at least, to land heavy guns for a bombardment. When he heard of delay in attacking, he immediately hurried forward a reinforcement of two hundred and forty men on board a ship of the Royal Navy, called the *Swallows' Prize*, besides two brigs loaded with provisions ; but, when they reached Port Royal on the tenth of September, the Basin was empty. The French held the fort undisturbed.

On that very day, the last of the transports had reached Massachusetts, and landed her cargo of dejected and derided unfortunates. The three commissioners, especially, were made the butt of popular ridicule, and shouts of "The three Port Royal worthies," "The three champions," greeted them when they appeared in public.

In this defence Subercase had been assisted by the Indians, whose support had to be purchased by liberal allowances. The meagre supplies furnished by the Home Government, at that time impoverished by the European war, compelled him to make great personal sacrifices to retain their friendship. At times, he parted with his own clothing to satisfy their demands. The settlers had suffered loss of houses, cattle and crops at the hands of the English, and were encouraged to continue active resistance by promise of ample rewards; but the exhausted state of the French treasury put it out of his power to relieve even real distress. The capture of a prize laden with valuable goods enabled him, in some measure, to keep faith with the Indians at this juncture, and retain the good-will of the inhabitants, who were not ardent in their attachment to their flag, so long as it flew over them.

CHAPTER VII.

GOVERNOR SUBERCASE—NICHOLSON'S CAPTURE OF PORT ROYAL.

1707-1710.

The two attacks of 1707, led the French to anticipate a renewal of hostilities against Port Royal the next year. In the spring of 1708, Subercase began work in earnest to put the fort in a state of thorough repair. The man-of-war ship *Venus*, sent to relieve the *Hind*, built at Port Royal, was anchored fast under the fort, and her crew put at work on the fortifications. During the whole summer, two hundred and fifty extra hands were engaged in pushing forward needed operations. A bomb-proof powder magazine, capable of holding sixty thousand pounds of powder, was built of stone brought from France, five years before, at the request of Brouillan. A building eighty feet in length, was fitted up to replace the chapel destroyed by the English, and barracks were completed for the soldiers. While occupied with these measures for protection, Subercase did not neglect to project offensive movements. A swift sailing man-of-war was asked for to assist the *Venus* in capturing English ships, and attacking the wealthy colony of Rhode Island, which had joined Massachusetts against Port Royal, in 1707. He also undertook to build another war vessel himself on the stocks at Port Royal. Not discouraged by the failure of the French Government to render assistance, Subercase engaged the services of the privateersmen, who did great damage to English commerce on these coasts. The prizes taken by them caused a temporary plenty in the colony. In March, 1709, a corsair left her winter quarters at Port Royal, and returned, twelve days later, with four prizes loaded with wheat and corn. Another, commanded by a bold fellow called Morpain, brought in nine prizes after a ten days' cruise. Morpain was attacked by a coast guard vessel near Boston, but, after a hard fight, succeeded in capturing the vessel and killing one hundred of her crew. She was brought to Port Royal, with a number of prisoners.

Subercase, writing that year, 1708, says: "The privateers have desolated Boston, having captured and destroyed thirty-five vessels. It has had scarcity of provisions the whole year, because our corsairs and others from West Indies captured from them six barques, the greater part of which were loaded." Four hundred and seventy prisoners were that year brought into Port Royal. The crowded condition of the people, the lack of sanitary measures, and the intemperate habits of the sailors and soldiers, in this season of riotous abundance, brought on an epidemic of spotted fever, in the autumn of the year, from which over fifty died. Some of the prisoners gave tidings of the equipment of a great force at Boston, consisting of New England troops, who were to be assisted by a squadron of the Royal Navy. On receipt of this intelligence, Subercase sent word to Quebec, and gathered a force of one hundred and forty Indians and seventy-five militiamen from Grand Pré. Morpain was induced to lend his efficient aid to his needy countrymen, as he had done in 1707. The woods on both banks of the river were cut away, that they might not again form a shelter for the enemy. We find Subercase strongly urging an increase in the garrison, as he expected an attack in the spring (1709). Thus, with untiring energy, the brave-spirited soldier prepared for the last defence of the old stronghold. He saw the needs, but lacked the wherewithal to supply defects, while never ceasing to make the best use of available resources. Writing to the authorities at home, he says: "I am at the last of my stock of

paper, and without a secretary, and for two months past
suffering from pain which leaves me not one hour free."

While Subercase, racked with pain, and labouring under
disheartening burdens, was heroically endeavouring to prepare for the inevitable encounter, the people of New England
were assembling the crushing armament destined to lower the
flag of France finally from the ramparts of Port Royal.   The
man who was chiefly instrumental in equipping a force to
attack the French in Acadia was Samuel Vetch, from whom
history has strangely withheld the award of merited honour.
After experience in border service, in which he gained an
accurate idea of the state of affairs in New France, he went
to England, where he passed the year 1708, in pressing a
scheme for the conquest of Canada upon the British Ministry.   His mission was so successful, that he returned to
America, in the spring of 1709, with instructions to the
several Colonial Governors to provide their quotas of troops,
to be associated with five regiments of British regulars in
the proposed invasion.   A powerful fleet was to be despatched
from England as well.   The Governors readily responded to
his appeals, and arrangements were made for a land attack
on Canada by Colonel Nicholson, who had been Governor
of several colonies ; while the men of Rhode Island and
Massachusetts, under Vetch, now raised to the rank of
Colonel, were to attack Port Royal.   Preparations were
completed in New England in May, but, all summer long,
they awaited in vain the appearance of the promised British
fleet.   At last, in October, intelligence reached them that the
ships had been detained for service in the Spanish war, thus
leaving the colonists to suffer a bitter disappointment and a
heavy financial burden.   Very soon after, Colonels Vetch and
Nicholson were sent to England to urge the Ministry to
further efforts.   As a result of their solicitations, a fleet was

sent out to Boston, in the summer of 1710, to join the colonists in an attack on Port Royal.

At last, on the twenty-ninth September, 1710, the expedition started on its voyage from the favourite anchorage at Nantasket. It consisted of thirty-six transports, protected by four ships of sixty guns each, two of forty guns, one of thirty-six, and two bomb galleys. Nicholson was General of the force, with Vetch second in command, in the capacity of Adjutant-General. There was one regiment of Marines, under Colonel Reading, and four New England regiments, commissioned by Queen Anne, and armed at her expense. They were commanded by Colonels Sir Chas. Hobby and Taylor of Massachusetts, Whiting of Connecticut, and Walton of New Hampshire. The Grenadiers of Walton's regiment were led by Paul Mascarene, afterwards Governor at Annapolis. This overpowering armament appeared at the entrance to the Basin about noon on Sunday, October fifth, and before night, came to an anchorage above Goat Island. The transport, *Caesar*, struck on the rocks in entering the passage, and during the night went to pieces, with a loss of twenty-six lives.

Subercase was in no position to hold Port Royal against so formidable a force. He had under him fewer than three hundred men, three-fourths of whom were raw levies from the cities of France, destitute of military training, and completely lacking in enthusiasm. He did not consider it safe to send them far from the fortifications, for fear of desertion, and for the same reason, was compelled to remove the boats and canoes ordinarily used for crossing the river. Provisions were scarce and prices high, even in autumn. The outlook was certainly unpromising to the man, who had reached the limit of personal credit. His own pathetic words disclose the dire extremity to which he was reduced: "I have had means by

my industry to borrow wherewith to subsist the garrison these
two years. I have paid what I could, by selling all my mov-
ables; I will give even to my last shirt, but I fear that all my
pains will prove useless, if we are not succoured."

Under these circumstances, most men would have bowed to
the inevitable, and at once capitulated; but the haughty spirit
of Subercase could not yield without a struggle, even against
overwhelming odds. Summoning the militia of the settlement to his assistance, and gathering the non-combatants of
the town within the walls, he determined to withstand the foe.
The British began to land on both shores, on the morning of
October sixth, and finding no force at hand to oppose them,
disembarked their whole army. Nicholson and Redknap, with
the commands of Reading, Hobby and Whiting, took the
south shore, while Vetch and Engineer Forbes, with Taylor's
and Walton's regiments, followed the Granville side. The
heavy guns on the water battery, and the mortars, thundered
volley after volley against the distant red coats, without
inflicting serious loss. Nicholson's men encamped that night
at a place he calls the "Brick Kilns," and, on the morning of
the seventh, struck through the woods, in a straight line for
the ford at Allen's Creek, in order to avoid the fire from the
fortifications. Anticipating resistance at the crossing, Nicholson sent a party of Indian scouts, supported by a detachment
of Marines, to clear the woods ahead. When this was done,
the General led his regiment of Grenadiers down the hill and
across the marsh, in full sight of the fort, with drums beating
and banners flying. On ascending the hill, after crossing the
stream, the French fired on them from their entrenched position in the woods, but were driven back by force of numbers
to the shelter of the fort. The Grenadiers halted on the crest
of Bailey Hill about noon, to await the arrival of the remainder of the army. Across the level, a mile away, rose the
grassy mounds of the French fort, surmounted with the

barking dogs of war. These spoke in decided tones, in the afternoon, when the British advanced down the slope towards the fort, harassed, as well, by musketry fire from cover of cottage, fence or garden. The main body soon halted, but an advance guard of Grenadiers and Marines entrenched themselves within four hundred yards of the works, in a position to cover the landing of stores at the shore, near the present brick-yard. When night came on, the garrison were treated to an entertainment of a novel and startling character. The bomb vessels of the fleet moved within range, and began to throw shells into the defences, to the consternation of the women and helpless refugees.

An attempt was also made at midnight by Colonel Vetch to plant a mortar battery opposite the fort, on the Granville shore; but, owing to unforeseen difficulties, the undertaking failed. When the garrison were busily engaged in replying to the fire of the bomb vessels, a number of boats, loaded with artillery, succeeded in getting up stream past the fort in the darkness. During the next four days, Subercase saw the toils surely tightening around him. Each night witnessed a grand display of artillery practice, the roar and flash of the discharge being mingled with the more terrible and deadly scream of the bursting shells. Shielded by this commotion, flotillas of boats were bearing material to General Nicholson for conducting a siege. On the Granville shore, one regiment held ground opposite the fort, and another was entrenched at the Narrows above, where communication was easily held with General Nicholson by night. The English refrained from assault; but were eagerly throwing up batteries, digging trenches, mounting cannon, placing mortars, while the guns on the land defences of Port Royal poured incessant showers of iron hail upon them. The French Governor, also, had roving bands of Indians and rangers prowling on the outskirts of the English camp, where they did effective service in cutting off stragglers.

Finally, on Sunday, October twelfth, Engineers Redknap
and Forbes announced that their preparations for siege operations were completed. These seem to have included a battery
of heavy guns on Bailey Hill, a mortar battery nearer the
works, and a battery of twenty-four Coehorn mortars, mounted
within one hundred yards of the walls. These last were a new
invention for throwing grenades, and considered very deadly.
All that October morning, the walls of the old fort at Port
Royal were shaken by the thunderous discharge of artillery.
A murderous fire of ball, shell and bursting grenade rained
upon the devoted few, who stood manfully to their guns, in a
contest that could have but one termination. When the fire of
the besiegers abated, two English officers were seen approaching the fort by way of Dauphin Street, bearing a flag of truce.
These were met by a party of French, who, after blindfolding
them, led them in at the gate, over the bridge, to the quarters
of the Governor. They bore a summons to Subercase to
surrender. The heroic General, who had seen his forces
weakened by repeated desertions, and whose ears were constantly assailed with the clamours of the inhabitants under his
protection, called a council of his officers, and, after consulta-
tion, agreed to treat with the enemy.

Hostilities ceased, for a few days, while terms were being
discussed, until, on the sixteenth of October, 1710, the keys of
the fort at Port Royal were handed by the gallant Subercase
to his conqueror. The scene enacted on that Thursday afternoon, within the gates of the old fort, was impressive in itself,
but especially memorable, because prophetic of a day, half a
century later, when the flag of France should be lowered for
the last time on the Continent of America. After an interview
of a subordinate with Subercase in the morning, respecting
details, General Nicholson, accompanied by Colonel Vetch
and all his field officers in splendid uniform, rode through the
gateway between lines of British Grenadiers under Mascarene

and others. With them came two French officers held as hostages, Bonaventure and Goutin. The French Governor met them half way on the bridge, accompanied by his officers and the two English hostages, Colonel Reading and Captain Mathews. With phrases complimentary to the conduct of a generous foe, he delivered the keys of the fort and magazines to Nicholson, completing his remarks with the significant expression, "hoping to give you a visit next spring." Nicholson at once handed the keys to Colonel Vetch, who held commission from Her Majesty to become the first Governor of her possession of Annapolis Royal in Nova Scotia. Governor Subercase, his officers and troops, wretchedly clothed, and bearing marks of bitter privation, marched out of the fort with all the honours of war, saluting the English General as they passed through the lines, on their way to the water side. The British marched into the fort, hoisted the Union Jack, and drank the Queen's health, with a royal salute, while the men-of-war and transports fired salvos from the river. Captain Mascarene mounted the first guard with sixty men. The French garrison, in accordance with the terms of surrender, were conveyed to France in British ships, while the settlers within three miles of the fort were permitted to remain in undisturbed possession of their lands for two years, on taking the oath of allegiance to the British crown; those at greater distance remained on suffrance.

A garrison of two hundred marines, and two hundred and fifty New England militia, remained to protect British interests. In recognition of divine aid in the capture, Tuesday, October twenty-first, was proclaimed a day of public thanksgiving. The first English service held in this Province was that day conducted in the chapel by the garrison chaplain, Rev. John Harrison. On Sunday, October twenty-sixth, General Nicholson boarded ship and left the river, but the fleet remained below Goat Island until the thirtieth, when it sailed for Boston.   At a Council of War, held on the twenty-third, a proclamation was made, in the name of the Queen, forbidding trade with any other portion of Nova Scotia save Annapolis Royal, which was intended to be made the "Port of Commerce" for the whole Province.

CHAPTER VIII.

FIGHTING AROUND ANNAPOLIS—TREATY OF UTRECHT—CONDITION
OF PEOPLE AND AFFAIRS DURING THE PEACE.

1710-1744.

At the time of the capture of Port Royal, Vaudreuil was
Governor of Canada. He was not insensible to the value of
Acadia, and, doubtless, would have made an attempt to recover it, had the condition of Canada permitted. He did the
best he could, under the circumstances, in sending Baron St.
Castin to keep alive the loyalty of the Acadians. The priests
also were incited to redouble their zeal in retaining the affec-
tion of the Indians. Special efforts on the part of the Canadian authorities were scarcely required, as the inhabitants of
the peninsula observèd a sullen attitude towards their con-
querors. We infer, from the fragmentary accounts of that
period, that the neighbouring French and Indians gave the
New England garrison little rest during the early period of
their occupation. In attempting to enforce authority over
those living at a distance, disputes frequently arose, leading to
bloodshed and imprisonment. The condition of the fort soon
grew bad, and sickness broke out among the soldiers. As
often as the English made attempts to conciliate the Indians,
all their efforts were frustrated by the missionary priests, who
had spent their lives among the tribes and had a potent
influence over them.

The inhabitants were ordered to bring in timber for the
purpose of making repairs on the fort ; but the native Indians,
supported by a band of hostiles from Maine, led by Castin,
prevented any response on the part of the people. When the
officer in command at Annapolis Royal was apprised of the

difficulty in securing the necessary timber, he sent a detachment of eighty men, under a captain, to surprise some families of Indians up the river, and seize the principal inhabitants. The Indians, learning of their approach, laid an ambuscade and killed thirty of the party, including the engineer and fort major. The remainder were taken prisoners. This action took place in the summer of 1711, at a place now called Bloody Creek, about twelve miles above Annapolis. The Acadians and Indians were elated at their success. Those who resided within the three-mile limit withdrew their families and flocks to a safe distance, on the plea that the recent action of the commander released them from their oaths. This bold action was prompted by the enfeebled state of the garrison, which was reduced to one hundred and twenty men, led now by Sir Charles Hobby, in the absence of Governor Vetch. St. Castin and the missionary, Gaulin, saw their opportunity. Hastily gathering a force of two hundred French and Indians, they proceeded to invest Annapolis, at the same time sending urgent appeals for assistance to the Governors of Canada and Placentia. Vaudreuil sent at once two hundred picked men with twelve officers, but was forced to recall them instantly to defend his own citadel ; while the gallant Morpain, whom the Governor of Placentia had sent with men, arms, and stores, had the misfortune to fall into the hands of a British man-of-war. Had this aid reached the French, Annapolis must have fallen into the hands of the resolute Acadian peasantry, who looked with bitter resentment on the occupation of their cherished heritage by an alien race. But fortune had flown to the side of the defenders ; and the besiegers, destitute of ordnance, and weary of waiting for expected help, sullenly withdrew from the fort when reinforcements to the garrison arrived from New England.

On the termination of operations against Canada, in the autumn of 1711, a force of four hundred British troops was sent to Annapolis. The arrival of these soldiers relieved the garrison from apprehension, and we do not read of further trouble during the remaining years of the war, which was terminated by the Treaty of Utrecht, April eleventh, 1713. In previous treaties England had shown a willingness to surrender American territory wrested from her antagonist. The New England Colonies having time and again seen the fruit of their hard earned conquests yielded by the Mother Country, now made energetic protests against a continuation of such a policy. Their representations were so urgent and unanswerable, that the Government resolved to end the policy of vacillation. Hence, in the Treaty of Utrecht, it was provided that all Acadia should be yielded to the Queen of Great Britain and to her Crown forever, together with Newfoundland, while France retained possession of the Island of Cape Breton, her " Isle Royale."

In 1714, General Nicholson was appointed Governor of Nova Scotia, and Commander-in-Chief of the forces. In a graceful letter addressed to him, the Queen expresses her wish that all French residents, who wish to continue in the country, should be allowed to retain their lands and tenements without molestation, or to sell them, if they chose to remove. This is held, naturally, to mean that the Acadian subjects of Her Majesty were placed upon an equal footing of rights and privileges with all others, and should assume like responsibilities. The French, however, seemed to interpret it otherwise. The agents of the Canadian French were ever present, in the priests, who received yearly pensions from the Governor of Quebec. These emissaries instilled into the minds of the people the idea that they were neutrals. The kind of neutrality intended was, that they should quietly aid the Indians against the English at all times, and, when England and France were at war, give aid to French incursions from Canada. They seemed to think they had done more than their duty to the English, if they did not take an open and active part in war against the garrison at Annapolis.

· Father Pain, missionary at Grand Pré, in writing to Governor Costabelle, in 1713, clearly expresses the prevailing sentiment. Speaking for the people, he says: "We shall answer for ourselves and for the absent, that we will never take the oath of allegiance to the Queen of Great Britain, to the prejudice of what we owe to our King, to our country, and to our religion." Costabelle had asked them to abandon their homes in Nova Scotia, and remove to Cape Breton, where France had begun the erection of the great fortress of Louisburg. Most of the Acadians were unwilling to exchange the rich fields of the peninsula for the rocky soil of Cape Breton, but they gave the Governor to understand that, though they were under the British flag, they still remained faithful subjects to the King of France.

On the accession of George First, commissioners were sent from Annapolis in a sloop of war to proclaim the King, and administer the oath of allegiance to the French inhabitants at Grand Pré, Chignecto and other places. The people refused to take the oath, on the pretext that they intended to leave the country. A year later, they were summoned to Annapolis before Lieutenant-Governor Caulfield, but were still unwilling to take the oath. In 1717, his successor, Lieutenant-Governor Doucett, asked the inhabitants of Annapolis to sign a declaration, acknowledging the King of Great Britain to be sole King of Acadia, and promising to obey him, as his true and lawful subjects. The French of Annapolis sent a written answer, that they were willing to comply, when provided with means of shelter against the savages, who were more friendly to the French than to the English. They expressed their willingness, moreover, to promise to bear arms against neither the King of England nor the King of France. Colonel

Phillips, Nicholson's successor, arrived at Annapolis, in 1720, but even the presence of the chief failed to induce the stubborn peasantry.

A little later, when the Governor sent agents with a proclamation to the various settlements, ordering the Acadians to take the oath, they not only refused, but are said to have written the French Governor of Louisburg, asking his aid. As Governor Phillips spent most of his time in England, the task of winning the allegiance of the French devolved upon his subordinates, the Lieutenant-Governors, resident at Annapolis. In 1726, Lieutenant-Governor Armstrong induced the settlers along the Annapolis River to take a qualified oath, in which there was a clause excusing them from bearing arms. When it again became necessary to ask for a declaration of fidelity, on the accession of George Second, in 1727, they refused to take the oath, except on conditions that were not deemed admissible by the authorities. Three of the principal men, who had been elected as deputies by the inhabitants, were at this time imprisoned by the Lieutenant-Governor for the influence they exerted in opposing his wishes. The question of taking the oath was, for a time, set at rest, when Governor-in-Chief Phillips visited the province in December, 1729. He succeeded in getting all the inhabitants to take an oath of allegiance with no reservation in regard to bearing arms. Governor Phillips was somewhat elated over his success in administering an unconditional oath, but the French affirm, with emphasis, that the verbal assurance of the Governor was given, that they should never be called upon to bear arms.

The attitude of the Acadian French was, in some measure, due to the insecure condition of the fort at Annapolis. Governor Vetch sent a memorial to the British Board of Trade, representing the bad state of the garrison, where the officers had been compelled to support and clothe the men. Hobby and Armstrong made similar representations, but met with slight response from the home authorities. The French inhabitants would not assist in effecting repairs, if they could avoid it, and, when summoned to provide timber for the fort, made plausible excuses. Paul Mascarene, writing as an engineer in 1720, said that the battery of large guns on the counterscarp of the ravelin, together with the ravelin itself, had been neglected by the English and allowed to go to ruin. He informs us, that the walls all around were revetted with timber eighteen feet long, to the height of the cordon, above which was placed the parapet of sod; yet in spite of constant repairs, the rain would cause breaches, owing to the sandy nature of the soil. In 1725, Armstrong states: "The barracks and other buildings are mouldering away, and if not speedily repaired, the garrison will be without lodgment, provision or defence." When Colonel Phillips was appointed Governor of Placentia and Nova Scotia, in 1717, he was placed in command of the 40th Regiment, of which six companies were to be stationed at Annapolis and four in Newfoundland. This Regiment remained on the station until the settlement of Halifax, in 1749, when Sir Edward Cornwallis succeeded Phillips as Colonel.

The years 1722-1725 were full of anxiety to the isolated garrison at Annapolis. The Indians from the Kennebec to Canso were on the war path against the English colonists, while remaining steadfast friends of the French. After raiding the fishing station at Canso, they succeeded in capturing several coasting craft and inflicting serious damage. Mr. Newton, collector at Annapolis, and two companions were made prisoners on their way to Boston. The Indians succeeded in getting possession of a vessel loaded with bread for the garrison at Annapolis, and, at once, formed the project of surrounding the fort and starving them out, as the English could not rely upon the Acadians for a supply of provisions. Governor Phillips, who happened to be at Canso at the time, forwarded a supply in time to relieve his hungry troops. Lieutenant-Governor Doucett, in command at Annapolis, succeeded in capturing a number of the enemy and broke up the investment.

In 1724, a large band of Malicetes and Micmacs, who had been camping at Isle Haute, suddenly appeared before Annapolis. A party sent to dislodge them were forced back into the fort, with the loss of several of their number. In reprisal for the scalping of the slain, the English killed and scalped an Indian prisoner, an act of wanton cruelty quite in keeping with the ferocious spirit that actuated both parties. After a time, the Indians and English concluded a treaty of peace, which was signed at Boston, in 1725, and formally ratified the next year at Falmouth, Maine, by the Governor of Massachusetts and New Hampshire, and Paul Mascarene from Annapolis on behalf of the English, and upwards of forty chiefs representing the Indians. A band of natives from the Upper St. John visited Annapolis, in 1728, to make submission to the Government. After being hospitably entertained by the Lieutenant-Governor, they were sent home well satisfied.

On the arrival of Governor Phillips, in 1720, councillors were chosen to assist him in the administration of affairs. These met for the first time in the house of Lieutenant-Governor Doucett in the garrison. Their names were John Doucett, Lawrence Armstrong, Paul Mascarene, Rev. John Harrison, Cyprian Southack, Arthur Savage, Hibbert Newton, William Skene, William Sheriff, Peter Boudre. Three days after, the name of John Adams was added, the only civilian member. In 1723, three English justices of the peace were appointed, and a justice and constable chosen from among the French population.

The number of English families living in Annapolis, about the year 1720, was but twelve, and these, for protection, had their residences near the fort. The French had gradually extended their settlement up the river, along its entire length. They had built dykes along its lower course to keep out the tides, and the land thus protected yielded immense crops of wheat, barley, roots and grass. At this period, the French had scarcely touched the heavily wooded upland, except for the purpose of cutting spars, for which they found ready sale. They are described as a frugal people, very industrious, and fond of hoarding the coin which they obtained in exchange for their products.

Accounts of proceedings in those early days are rare ; but we, now and again, find reference to some transaction that serves to give a glimpse of life in old Annapolis Royal. We read that, under the French *regime*, in the days of Subercase, the reluctant soldiers were called out on the parade ground to shoot a comrade convicted of murder. After the execution, his body was exposed to the gaze of passers by. In 1725, the Council passed sentence on a servant of Governor Armstrong for insulting his master. The terms would to-day, be considered onerous for a similar offence : " The punishment therefore inflicted on thee, is to sit upon a gallows three days, one half hour each day, with a rope about thy neck and a paper upon your (*sic*) breast, whereon shall be wrote ' Audacious Villain ' ; and afterwards, thou art to be whipt at a cart's tail from the prison up to the uppermost house of the Cape, and from thence back again to the prison house, receiving each one hundred paces five stripes upon your bare back, with a cat-of-nine-tails."

On April tenth, 1734, the officers of the garrison of Annapolis Royal petitioned that the small enclosure, adjoining the Governor's garden and the White House field, and lying opposite the fort gate, should be reserved and set apart for them and their successors as a bowling green forever. The bowling green is now covered with the residences of our citizens, but our youth find an unrivalled green within the ramparts of the noble fort, that was for centuries the abode of military energy. No longer is heard the tread of the tireless sentinel or his challenging cry. The glacis is deserted now, save by the curious visitor, who wanders with thoughtful tread over ground hallowed by so many stirring memories.

Lieutenant-Governor Armstrong had difficulty in arranging the claims of the La Borgne family to fees and rents of lands, on ground of seigneurial rights. The matter resolved itself, finally, into a litigation between Madame Belleisle and her son on the one side, and Mrs. Agatha Campbell and the D'Entremonts on the other. In 1732, the other claimants sold their rights to Mrs. Campbell, who was grand-daughter of Charles La Tour and Madame D'Aunay. Mrs. Campbell conveyed these rights to the British Crown for the sum of three thousand guineas. The Crown appointed collectors to gather the rents from the settlers, but the amount realized was small, as many refused to acknowledge the claim of any Seigneur. Attempts were made at this time to fix definite boundaries to the farms, in regard to which matters were in great confusion.

While the English were eking out a precarious existence at Annapolis, French power was increasing wonderfully on the island of Cape Breton. The great fortress of Louisburg was being constructed, at enormous expense, to safeguard the interests of France in the New World. The people from the French colony of Placentia had removed to Louisburg, and had succeeded in controlling the trade of Nova Scotia. The Acadian peasantry at Chignecto, Grand Pré, and even Anna-polis, had as little intercourse as possible with the British, so that the garrison at Annapolis Royal was dependent upon New England for most of their supplies. Boston was head-quarters for the English of Annapolis. There, all bills were negotiated, and from that vicinity most of the English-speaking residents came. The trade between the two places was carried on by four or five sloops, which brought West Indian products and English manufactured goods, taking away furs and feathers as the staple exports. About 1720, the trade in the last mentioned articles was upwards of £10,000 per year, figures which show the place to have been a great centre for Indian supply. On the death of Lieutenant-Governor Armstrong, in 1739, Paul Mascarene succeeded to the office. He was a French Huguenot, who had been driven from his country by religious persecution. Entering the British army, he raised himself by his own exertions to the high position of Major-General. He had been a captain under Nicholson in 1710, and soon afterwards breveted Major. We have seen him commanding the first guard mounted at Annapolis Royal. On the death of Lieutenant-Colonel Cosby, in 1742, he became resident commander of the regiment, as well as administrator of the colony. Governor Mascarene assumed control at a time when a strong hand was needed to direct affairs at Annapolis. Peace had prevailed for many years between the mother countries in Europe, but an ill-concealed feeling of hostility animated the breasts of their descendants in America. The unremitting activity of French agents from Louisburg and Quebec kept alive the slumbering fires of resentment in the hearts of the Acadian people. The time was approaching when the restraining leashes would be slipped, and the land again desolated by the mad ravages of war. It was the time, before the tempest's shock, to make all secure, and Mascarene took immediate measures to strengthen his defences.

For twenty years, we find little mention of the fort at Annapolis, but, from its subsequent condition, it was probably undergoing a process of slow decay. In 1733, a ship arrived from London, bringing cannon, carriages and ordnance stores · from the Tower. This ship also brought workmen to put the garrison and outworks in repair. The storehouses and magazine were spoken of as not being bomb-proof. The repairs effected at that time must have been but temporary, as, about 1740, complaints were urged respecting the breaches in the walls, owing to the looseness of the soil and the decay of the revetting timber. The engineers sent out by the Board of Ordnance reported against attempting further repairs on the earthworks, and recommended a fortification of stone and brick, on the original lines. Preparations were made in accord with this report. For two years, large quantities of stone, brick and lime were gathered in readiness for construction, while no attention was given to the crumbling walls of the old defences. At this juncture, the Lords of Trade warned Governor Mascarene that war was likely to break out between England and France. Work on stone and brick was discontinued, and the artisans were at once employed in repairing the very defective earth walls of the fort. In this they were assisted by the Acadians, who brought the necessary timber and even joined in other labour, but their operations were destined to be rudely interrupted.

CHAPTER IX.

WAR OF AUSTRIAN SUCCESSION—STIRRING EVENTS IN ACADIA—
THREE ATTACKS ON ANNAPOLIS ROYAL.

1744-1748.

England declared war against France in April, 1744. The
French in Louisburg, under the leadership of Duquesnel, had
long been preparing for the struggle. M. du Vivier, a de-
scendant of Charles La Tour, had been an active agent in
stimulating the patriotism of the Acadians of Nova Scotia.
As far back as 1735, he had published a memoir, disclosing
the methods adopted to keep the people in close accord with
the French of Cape Breton. According to this, some of the
inhabitants of Annapolis, on whom the English placed greatest
reliance, were secretly inciting feelings of hostility among
their countrymen. The news of the declaration of war
reached Louisburg before the authorities at Annapolis got
intelligence of it from Boston. France had actually declared
war twenty-five days before the British. The ardent Du
Vivier at once asked for a force to capture the peninsula.
The Governor, knowing the weak state of the English garrison, gave Du Vivier three hundred men, with several armed
vessels, and told him to make his promises good. Sailing at
once to Canso, he captured the block-house at that place, with
its garrison of eighty men, May eleventh, 1744. Two hundred
Indians joined him at Canso. Had he pushed on at once to
Annapolis with his augmented force it would undoubtedly
have fallen. Its garrison consisted of but one hundred and
fifty men, insufficiently protected by its weakened walls.
The presence of a large number of women and children
would also have been a great incumbrance to the defence.

Previously to hostilities, the families of the soldiers could not be all accommodated in the fort, and were living in the village, as were also the English and New England workmen, engaged in preparing material for the new fort. But Du Vivier lingered at Canso, and gave his capable adversary time to adopt measures for more effective resistance.

News of the declaration of war had not reached Annapolis, when, on May eighteenth, a rumour spread in the lower town that Morpain, the famous privateersman, was up river with five hundred men. This created a panic, in which there was a general rush for the fort. This rumour, though false, put Mascarene on his guard, and in a measure prepared him to receive the news of war, which came a few days later. Three vessels were sent to Boston at once, conveying the families of the officers, but, even then, seventy women and children were left behind to brave the terrors of the coming storm. The engineers were vigorously pushing on repairs in the breaches of the old walls, and had succeeded in getting them into a state of tolerable efficiency, when a body of hostile Indians three hundred strong, led by young Belleisle and other Acadians, appeared in the neighbourhood. The French labourers at once ceased their work on the fortifications, and returned to their homes. These Indians had been with Du Vivier at Canso, and had preceded him to Grand Pré, where they were to await his arrival before advancing against Annapolis. The anxiety of Belleisle to win the honour of recapturing the home of his ancestors, coupled, no doubt, with feelings of rivalry against Du Vivier as representing a foreign French element, led him to start alone. Accompanying Belleisle, and the guiding spirit in the movement, was a missionary priest named Le Loutre, a most determined enemy to the British.

The Indians appear to have pursued their usual tactics, in stealthily approaching the walls, before the guard was aware

of their presence. In this way they took the lives of two
men, and nearly succeeded in capturing a larger party,
engaged in demolishing buildings on the Governor's grounds.
They then found shelter behind some.small buildings near the
foot of the glacis, from which they kept up a fire of small
arms against the fort. They were soon dislodged from this
cover by the cannon of the defenders. Advancing next to
the lower town, one quarter of a mile from the fort, they
began to set fire to the houses in that direction. The flames
spread and threatened to consume the block-house, which
stood on Dauphin Street (St. George) where it was widest,
probably near the present post-office. The sergeant in charge
withdrew with his guard, but a rescuing party from the fort
boarded a small vessel, moved opposite the block-house and
opened fire upon the Indians. When these were driven off,
the men landed and proceeded to put out the fire, which had
not injured the block-house. Working parties from the
garrison then proceeded to level all buildings within musket
shot of the walls, which could serve as shelter for the lurking
savages. As these doughty warriors had no intention of
exposing their precious bodies to the artillery fire of the
English gunners, they wisely withdrew to the distance of one
mile, and satisfied themselves with stealing cattle and sheep
from the farmers in the neighbourhood. The Indians
appeared on July first; on the fifth a galley arrived from
Massachusetts with seventy militiamen to reinforce the
garrison. The Indians then retired to Grand Pré, without
having accomplished more than the destruction of a few
vacant houses. Governor Mascarene sent the wives and
children of his soldiers to Boston on the return of the
transport. Soon afterwards, forty more men were sent him by
Governor Shirley, an addition that enabled him to show a
respectable force, for whom, however, he experienced great
difficulty in providing serviceable weapons.

While these Indians were making their premature attack on Annapolis Royal, Du Vivier was encountering difficulties in his progress across the peninsula. He had gone by water to Chignecto, hoping to' find his compatriots in that section zealous supporters of his projects. In this expectation he was disappointed, as very few joined his ranks. Going next to Grand Pré, where the crest-fallen Indians were awaiting his arrival, he found the people still more unwilling to render him assistance. His haughty manner of demanding supplies, under threat of punishment, alienated the Acadians, who were indisposed to take any active part in proceedings that might bring upon them the reprisals of war. Advancing through the woods from Grand Pré, he reached the settlements on the Upper Annapolis about the end of August. The force under his command, consisted of two hundred soldiers and four hundred and fifty Indians. After resting for two days, they came down river and pitched camp on the brow of the hill, one mile from the fort, the very place where Nicholson's camp had been, in 1710.

Next morning they advanced towards the fort with colours flying, but retreated when they found the fire of the batteries growing too hot for them. Du Vivier then resorted to the plan of night attacks, keeping up a constant fire against the parapets, and wearying the garrison with repeated alarms. As there were many parts of the walls easy of access, and unprovided with palisades, the defenders were considerably annoyed. Du Vivier then tried to intimidate them with the declaration, that a strong French naval force was daily expected to support his attack, and demanded the surrender of the fort; but the brave Mascarene would not consent to a capitulation. The night attacks were kept up for three weeks, but were attended with little loss of life. During the day, the British gunners would occasionally drop a shot into the encampment of the enemy, as a reminder of their alertnesś. Tradition says that the French flag-staff was shot away, and that an Indian, standing on a high rock still to be seen on the hillside, was killed by a cannon ball. Du Vivier got scaling ladders ready for assaulting the works, and is said to have offered four hundred livres to every Indian who would mount the rampart, but his dusky allies were not responsive. While Mascarene was anxiously awaiting the issue, and even taking his place at night on the ramparts, fearing the arrival of the expected naval armament, his heart was cheered by a further reinforcement of fifty Indian rangers from Massachusetts. It is said that one of these Indians, falling into the hands of the French, told Du Vivier that Mascarene intended to attack his encampment the following night. This information had such an effect upon the valorous chief, that he at once broke camp, in which he had passed a whole month, and started in a driving rain storm for Grand Pré, where he hoped to pass the winter. The inhabitants of that settlement were so opposed to his wintering among them, that he withdrew to Chignecto, where he met with a similar reception. Dispirited by the indifference of the Acadians, he retired to Louisburg, to answer before his commander for the bad managemeut of the campaign.

A few days after Du Vivier's departure, a French frigate, with two other armed vessels, arrived in the Basin, but refrained from attacking the fort, when they were apprised of the withdrawal of Du Vivier. Two vessels from Boston with provisions for the garrison were captured by these ships. After lying at anchor three days inside the gap, they sailed away with their prizes. It was fortunate for Mascarene that the French flotilla was so late in reaching Annapolis, and that the Acadians were so indisposed to assist their country-men in arms. Had matters been otherwise, Annapolis Royal would certainly have fallen into the hands of the French at

that time. The Governor gratefully acknowledged the conduct of the inhabitants in his correspondence.

Although large quantities of material were gathered, no
further effort was made to construct a fort of stone. The
chief engineer was called home to New Hampshire, where a
French attack was apprehended. But Mascarene, an engineer
himself, hurried forward repairs upon his walls during the
autumn and winter, so that, by spring, his preparations for
attack were approaching completion. Indeed, he might have
looked with a feeling approaching complacency at the work
that had been accomplished, for there is no doubt, that at
no period in its history, had the fort at Annapolis Royal
presented defences of so formidable a character.

We gather the following interesting particulars from a
chronicle dated, June, 1745. "There are on the river battery
six twenty-four pounders, on the ramparts, one twelve-inch
mortar and thirty pieces of cannon. The wall is of earth,
faced with squared timbers ten by twelve inches, and eighteen
feet long, joined together and set up perpendicularly." The
cordon projected to overhang these timbers, and upon the
cordon was constructed the parapet of sodded earth. "The
top of the parapet is set off with round logs a foot in
diameter, fastened with rope at the ends. These logs are so
disposed as to admit of being loosened and slipped over the
talus of the parapet to break the ladders of a scaling party.
The ditch may be sixty to seventy feet in width, and thirty
to thirty-five feet in depth. In its centre is a cunette (a wet
ditch in the middle of a dry one) protected by a staked
palisade. The glacis, with well-defined salient and entering
angles, may be ninety feet. The outworks consist of three
block-houses; one situated between the mouth of the Allen
Creek and the fort, to defend the plain; the other two, east
north-east of the fort, defend the approach to the lower

Town. The most part of houses in Lower Town belong to officers of the garrison. The English, moreover, have a large frame house there to lodge their Indian allies," (Massachusetts Rangers, for whom there were no quarters available within the fort) "which is defended by four guns." The wooden timbers have disappeared, subsequent changes modified the character of the embankment, but the visitor who stands to-day on the ramparts of Annapolis Royal, with the above description in hand, will have no difficulty in comprehending the strength of Mascarene's fortification. He was freed from the worrying presence of helpless women and children, and with three hundred good men at his back, awaited what the opening season of 1745 might bring him.

The experience of the previous summer taught the English that they were liable to be attacked any day. Rumors of a gathering at Chignecto reached Annapolis as early as March, and, in May, an officer named Marin, with three hundred Canadians, and as many Indians gathered by the wily Le Loutre, appeared before the town. Marin had passed the winter at Chignecto, and had been kept informed of Mascarene's preparations by the Acadians of the valley. It is said that two boys, Charles Raymond and Peter Landry, made three journeys between Grand Pré and Annapolis, during the winter in the interests of Marin. On the enemy's approach, the English population deserted their houses and took refuge within the walls. Houses that might afford any protection to the foe were torn down. For three weeks, Marin maintained the investment, which was enlivened by an occasional night attack, in which neither party seems to have suffered severe loss. Two trading craft from Boston were captured and a few houses burned, but, beyond that, nothing worthy of note occurred. It is possible he might have continued the siege longer, had not an urgent summons from the Governor of Louisburg hastened his departure.

That stronghold, whence the haughty French had launched their ventures against the peace and quiet of the Valley of Annapolis, had, itself, now to experience the bitterness and humiliation of capture at the hands of a force of artisans, led by a civilian. On the afternoon of June seventeenth, 1745, Duchambois, the Governor, yielded possession of Louisburg to a New England garrison.

Although the Acadians adopted a neutral attitude towards Du Vivier and Marin, it is evident that their national feelings were aroused at this capture. They had, for years, driven a flourishing trade with their countrymen, in supplying the garrison at Louisburg with farm produce ; but, immediately upon the English assuming control, they ceased to take cattle or provisions, even to their own serious financial loss. The Indians continued to be actively hostile, and made every exertion to interrupt communication between Annapolis and the Louisburg garrison. Governor Mascarene, whose urbanity had won the confidence of many of the French peasantry, and whose French birth, no doubt, won him favour among them, looked with anxious concern at the evidences of growing unrest among this numerous population. He was convinced that France would not yield her pet fortress, without a further effort, and knew well that the retention of Annapolis Royal by the British, depended mainly upon the attitude of the large body of Acadian French peasantry. Aware of the critical state of affairs, he asked for a ship of war to act as guard and convoy, and for a tender to carry dispatches and enforce order among the people up the Bay, whose conduct the year before had not pleased him. The Government, in answer to this request, sent the ship of war *Dover* to Annapolis, in June 1746, where she was detained to resist an expected attack. The fears of Governor Mascarene were well founded. The French, both in the Old World and in the New, were aroused to one determined effort to recover their lost possessions in Acadia. An immense armament was fitted out at Brest, by far the most powerful that had ever prepared to cross the Atlantic. Its purpose was to restore French ascendency, wherever the French flag had floated in America, and inflict severe chastisement, as well, upon the pestilent shopkeepers of New England.

The story of this fated expedition is well known. A fleet of seventy ships left France, carrying thirteen thousand men. Of this proud array, forty-two, battered by storm and wave, reached Chebucto, Halifax. There, a pestilence broke out among the crowded troops, which carried off between two and three thousand men. Their leader, Duke d'Anville, sickened and died. His successor, D'Estournelle, driven to distraction by the horrors about him, committed suicide. La Jonquiere, the new Governor of Canada, then took command, and des- pairing of capturing Louisburg with his weakened force, resolved to sail for Annapolis, which was considered certain· prey. The fleet of over forty ships left Chebucto on the thirteenth October, 1746, prepared to crush any feeble opposi- tion possible to be offered. But success was not destined to crown even this effort. A storm met them off Cape Sable; more ships were disabled ; discouraging news of an English fleet reached the commander, who set his pilots on shore and turned the prows of his ships from the shores, where bleached the bones of so many brave comrades.

The Canadian Governor, Marquis de Beauharnois, had zealously seconded the project of recovering Acadia. M. de Ramesay was sent with a force of six hundred men, among them many colonial officers of distinction, for the purpose of arousing the Acadians in Nova Scotia to take vigorous action against the English at Annapolis Royal. Three hundred Malecite Indians joined him at Chignecto, and a large band of Micmacs, under the well-known leaders St. Pierre and

Marin. Two ships had been sent from France in advance of the great fleet, for the purpose of meeting Ramesay and joining him in an attack on Annapolis, but the naval commanders refused to accompany him before the arrival of their admiral. Ramesay finally grew weary of waiting and started for home, but was recalled by a runner, with the intelligence that the fleet was in Chebucto harbour. He retraced his steps, hastened to Grand Pré, and thence to Annapolis, where he arrived at the end of September with seven hundred men. Reinforcements had just arrived to the garrison from Boston, raising the garrison to five hundred men, while two British frigates and an armed schooner lay at anchor in the Basin. Ramesay acted a discreet part in refraining from any attack. He encamped at some distance, awaiting the approach of the invincible armada of France. It never came. When he heard of its departure from Cape Sable, he withdrew with his troops, first to Grand Pré, and afterwards to Chignecto, where he decided to pass the winter. The presence of these Canadians at Chignecto aroused the fears of Mascarene, who knew the influence they were having upon the inhabitants of that settlement, in awakening hopes of a reconquest of the country by France.

At Mascarene's request, the far-seeing and energetic Governor of Massachusetts sent over five hundred men, under Colonel Noble, to be stationed at Grand Pré, as a check to the French at the isthmus. The detachment landed on the shores of the Bay of Fundy, in the month of December, and forced its way over the mountain and through the woods to the Acadian settlement, at the mouth of the Gaspereau. While there, quartered on the inhabitants, and passing the time in careless unconcern, they were attacked, in the early morning of February tenth by the Canadians from Chignecto, led by De Villiers and La Corne. These courageous rangers of the woods had braved the perils of a winter journey across the wilds, to catch their foeman off his guard. They were completely successful. Having had exact information from the people of Pizequid, Windsor, respecting the quarters of the chief officers, they first attacked them. Colonel Noble, four of his officers, with seventy non-commissioned officers and men were killed, while struggling in the darkness against their unseen enemies. Sixty of the English were wounded, and sixty-nine taken prisoners. The remainder of the New Englanders made desperate efforts, during the morning, to reach their stores, but were not able to accomplish their object owing to the great depth of snow. Terms of surrender were finally agreed to, by which they were permitted to depart for Annapolis within forty-eight hours, carrying their arms and sufficient provisions. Mr. How, a member of the Council at Annapolis, was one of the prisoners taken at that time.

This lamentable occurrence was a sad blow to the British, but, in its ultimate consequences, more disastrous to the Acadian French. It inspired hopes within their breasts, and awoke ambitions, that no doubt influenced them at the crisis in their history, a few years later. Annapolis had breathed the air of suspense for three years. During all this time, its able and determined commander was foreseeing that events might occur, on any day, to awaken into fury the slumbering passions of the ten thousand French in Nova Scotia. Before such a blast, the few English in the province would, in a twinkling, be swept into the sea. To avert such a catastrophe, had been the constant aim of Mascarene in his delicate management of the simple minded and credulous, yet determined people. He well knew the powerful influence that had been wielded by the presence of the great fleet, even under the adverse conditions of the previous summer, and dreaded the return of the resolute Jonquiere with a fresh armament. His apprehensions were finally allayed by the defeat of another expedition under Jonquiere, which left Rochelle in May, 1747. Admirals Anson and Warren met this fleet off Cape Finisterre, and succeeded in annihilating it. Of thirty-eight ships but one escaped. This great victory broke the naval power of France, and at once relieved the English colonies in America from the dread of invasion. The Canadians, under Ramesay, had been ready to act in concert with Jonquiere, and had formed a project of capturing Annapolis, where the garrison were reported to be suffering from sickness during the summer. When they learned of Jonquiere's irreparable disaster, and knew that Governor Shirley had at once sent another force to occupy Grand Pré, they withdrew to Quebec. A small body under Marin were in the Province during 1748, but did not succeed in accomplishing more than some petty pillaging.

The reader has been able to see how much the English at Annapolis Royal owed to the energetic Governor of Massachusetts, during the eventful years of this war. On every occasion, when the hard pressed garrison were reduced to desperate straits, the arrival of succour from the friendly neighbourhood of Boston turned the tide. The readiness with which reinforcements were hurried forward, after the humiliating surrender at Grand Pré, shows the abiding faith of Governor Shirley in the ultimate value of the little peninsula of Nova Scotia. In acknowledgment of the warm interest manifested by him in Nova Scotia affairs, he was requested by the British Secretary of State to assist Governor Mascarene in the protection of the province from further assault. The assistance rendered was important from the financial standpoint, as the Governor at Annapolis had no means of collecting revenue, owing to the complete paralysis of trade.

In 1748, English diplomacy restored the island of Cape Breton to France by the Treaty of Aix-la-Chapelle. The people of New England, who had captured Louisburg at much cost, were incensed at its surrender. Its restoration to France was an egregious blunder, as no English settlement was secure, while that stronghold remained as a centre of French intrigue in America. Great Britain, however, disheartened at the result of the campaigns in Europe, and threatened with a repetition of the Jacobite troubles at home, was anxious for peace, while her ambitious rival clung with tenacious persistency to the recovery of the island, that guarded the portal to her Canadian domain. Both nations, at last, agreed to yield places captured during the war, and in return for the trading post of Madras, .in the East Indies, France, once more, occupied her old vantage ground in the west.

CHAPTER X.

ANNAPOLIS CEASES TO BE THE CAPITAL—EXPULSION OF ACADIANS.

1748-1775.

At the time of the Treaty of Aix-la-Chapelle, the English had been in possession of Nova Scotia for nearly forty years ; but, with the exception of the fishing post at Canso, not a single settlement had been formed by them. The attitude of the Micmacs had been so invariably hostile, that isolated residence by a New Englander in any part of the province, was out of the question ; and, upon the outbreak of war in 1744, those who lived in the vicinity of the fortifications of Annapolis Royal returned to New England, or sought shelter behind the walls, from time to time, as occasion demanded. Governor Shirley, with characteristic promptitude, proposed to establish New England colonists among the French, in such numbers as to be able to hold their own in an emergency ; but this practical suggestion of securing a resident English population was not acted upon. The French Acadians, on the other hand, had gone on steadily increasing in numbers and making substantial increase in resources. In 1748, they were three times as numerous as in 1710, and it may be said quite as warmly sympathetic to French interests. The few years of conflict had quickened aspirations, which had for many years lain dormant, as well as aroused antagonism to the exercise of authority by the dominant power.

From the discovery of the country, the chief interest had centred in the colony at Port Royal. It is true that the other French settlements had become more populous, but they were the offspring of the parent colony, and recognized it as the centre of authority and influence. Under British rule, as well, the history of the province, until 1749, is the history of Annapolis Royal. Here resided the Governor, the commanders of the forces, the garrison with its numerous accessories. The members of the council, who had in hand the administration of the province, lived in Annapolis. Here gathered all who sought safety in time of danger, as well as those who came to barter in times of peace. Annapolis Royal was called upon to surrender this position, in 1749, when Governor Cornwallis arrived at Chebucto with a number of disbanded soldiers, for the purpose of forming a settlement on the shores of that magnificent harbour. A plan for carrying into effect the long cherished design of planting a town on Chebucto harbour was matured by the Board of Trade and Plantations, in 1748. A large number of military and naval officers and men embarked, in May, 1749, on a fleet of thirteen ships, under the leadership of the Honourable Edward Cornwallis, who had superseded Phillips as Governor of Nova Scotia. The first ship arrived at Chebucto, June twenty-first, old style, and soon afterward was followed by the entire fleet without mishap. Lieutenant-Governor Mascarene and his council were summoned from Annapolis, to meet his superior in the new town of Halifax, so called after Lord Halifax, the President of the Board of Trade. On Friday, July twenty-fifth, the Civil Government was organized, by swearing in as Councillors, on board the ship *Beaufort*, Colonel Paul Mascarene, Captain Edward Howe, Captain John Gorham, Benjamin Greene, John Salsbury and Hugh Davison, the first three being of the Annapolis Garrison. The forma-tion of the Board was announced to the people by a general salute from the ships, and the day was made a public holiday. It is worthy to note that the table, around which this first council sat, is still in use in the Province Building at Halifax. After an absence of six weeks, Lieutenant-Governor Mascarene returned to the command of the garrison at Annapolis. As the large and flourishing French ·Acadian settlement of Grand Pré lay between Annapolis and · Halifax, measures were at once taken to place an armed force there for security of communication. One of ·the block-houses at Annapolis was taken down and erected at Grand Pré, while one hundred men of the garrison were sent to defend it, and prevent the people from sending their cattle out of the province.

Nothing of material interest is to be noted at Annapolis, for the next few years. The watchful Mascarene was ever on the alert to meet the wily stratagems of the Indians, and the persistent efforts of the Canadian French to occupy and hóld the western shores of the Bay of Fundy, on the ground that the Acadia, ceded to Britain, was the peninsula only. In 1750, a flotilla of small craft took on material at Annapolis for the construction of barracks and block-houses on the Isthmus of Chignecto, as the French were getting very troublesome in that vicinity. The Canadians replied to this, by the construction of a strong fort on a small stream, which they claimed as the boundary between the territories of the two nations. The British were now reaping the result of their vacillating policy of take and return, so long played with the French in America. The sagacious leaders of New France had pursued, with relentless determination, the fixed purpose of keeping the English within the bounds of the Alleghanies. Although the French Canadians were few, compared with the numerous colonists of England, in America, they responded much more readily to the control of an authoritative leader, and dared to dictate terms to the prosperous Atlantic Provinces. The dream which La Galissonniere and Du Quesne hoped to see realized, was a French domain stretching from the St. Lawrence to the Mississippi mouth. The Ohio was to be theirs ; the Illinois also ; Lakes George and Champlain in their keeping ; the noble expansion of the Canadian lakes,

7

the waterway of the St. John and the Isthmus of Chignecto were to be held secure ; all dominated by strongholds, whose names have become familïar to every school boy in the country. Ticonderoga, Crown Point, Du Quesne, Beausejour, ring in our ears to-day, and sound the knell of hopes, cherished with such fervour, by those zealous and patriotic leaders of New France. When the English saw the French erecting forts on the St. John and the Isthmus, in territory which was claimed to be British, they took immediate steps to secure their removal by force. The authorities at Halifax and New England joined in an expedition against Fort Beausejour, on the Isthmus of Chignecto.

Although England and France did not declare war until 1756, their zealous offspring in America were pommelling each other, all the year 1755. A fleet left Boston, in May of that year, bearing a force of English and colonial troops under command of Colonel Monckton. It called at Annapolis, where three hundred infantry and a small train of artillery joined it. After a siege of two weeks, Beausejour, and a smaller fort at Bay Verte, with a large number of prisoners, were captured. Among these, were many Acadians, who had been forced into service, or had been beguiled by the plausible representations of the artful Le Loutre.

A few months later, saw the gathering of a flotilla in the Basin for a different purpose. The day of darkness and disaster had come for the perverse and deluded inhabitants of the broad vales of Acadia. Again and again, had Governor Cornwallis invited them to accept the lot of citizens of a free country, to share the burden of responsibility, as well as enjoy the protection of strong government. The oath of allegiance was submitted to them, time after time, the consequences of refusal were distinctly stated ; yet, in defiance to friendly advice and kindly overtures, they plainly declared their preference for exile. Space forbids discussion on this fruitful theme. England was about to enter into a death grapple with France, in which the odds were plainly not in her favour. It was no time for half measures. She had, at some time, to assert her sovereignty in Nova Scotia, and obtain security for her own sons, which the alien tendencies of these self-styled neutrals rendered impossible. Situated midway between the French centres of mischievous influence in Cape Breton and Canada, no reliance could be placed upon these people in the re-opening of warlike enterprises. Their removal must not be looked upon as the outcome of fixed and definite purpose, on the part of a government carrying out its ordinary policy in time of peace ; but must be regarded as an act of expediency, necessary for self-preservation, reluctantly determined upon by responsible leaders, in a dire emergency, amid the anxieties of impending war. Whatever opinion we may entertain concerning the righteousness of the judgment, that sent them into exile, few—in this land that has been watered with their tears—can withhold the meed of sympathy from · those wretched peasants, who suffered a tenfold retribution for their dogged refusal to accept the terms of the British Governor.

"'Tis true; 'tis pity; yet pity 'tis, 'tis true." Measures were taken by Governor Lawrence, without the formal sanction of the British Government, to remove the Acadian people to the different English colonies. Major Handfield, who was in command at Annapolis, was informed that transports would be sent to him from Boston to convey one thousand persons, of whom three hundred would be sent to Philadelphia, two hundred to New York, three hundred to Connecticut, and two hundred to Boston. Handfield's instructions bade him use measures of compulsion, and to deprive any, who should escape, of all means of shelter and support, by burning their houses, and destroying everything that could afford means of subsistence. He was informed that Colonel Winslow would march across from Grand Pré, with a strong detachment, to pick up stragglers, and that any ship, which had not received her complement of passengers up the Bay, would call at Annapolis. Not long after he had received his instructions, the ships came, prepared for their living freight. Not a huge Armada, certainly, but destined to be freighted with such a burden of sorrow. The names of a few vessels have come down to us. There was the ship *Hopson*, the sloops *Sarah and Molly*, *Dolphin*, *Hannah*, *Three Friends* and *Swan*; names innocent enough, but ominous to the startled inhabitants of this quiet valley, who were summoned to hear the fateful decree of banishment. The task set before the military was a very difficult one. To gather so scattered a people, and place them on the transports was almost an impossibility. Many abandoned their homes, on getting intelligence of the intentions of the Government, and fled to the woods for safety, and much difficulty was experienced in securing them. Some of these refugees crossed the South Mountain, back of Bridgetown, and built huts in the woods, where, to-day, we may find remains of pottery, in evidence of their lonely residence. Hunger, finally, compelled most of them to surrender, and upwards of eleven hundred souls were placed on board vessels at Annapolis Royal.

In the season of clear skies and balmy air, the charming month of September, these devoted people were torn away from homes that were sacred by the hallowed associations of long years of industry and privation. With hearts wrung with anguish, they saw the merciless flames devour the very shrines of their devotion ; saw their barns and granaries, that were bursting with the offerings of a generous harvest, reduced to blackened ashes ; heard the plaintive lowing of their cattle, the bleating of their flocks, the mournful lament of the faithful watch-dog beside the dying embers of the desolated hearth ;

but yet they lived. They lived, to carry into distant lands and other scenes, the echoes that rung in their ears, and the memories that burned in their bfains, while reason held her throne, and the pulse of life throbbed in their bosoms. The impulse to escape was strong upon them, even when on their voyage. One craft, which was carrying more than two hundred into exile, was captured by her passengers and taken into the St. John, where the Acadians joined their Canadian countrymen. After reaching their various destinations, they at once began making attempts to return. Some were sent to the West Indies, whose climate was fatal; some to England, where they took the oath of allegiance, and, after a time, regained a footing in Acadia. Others again, on hired craft, coasted the New England shores in hopes of regaining possession of their old homes, so that, in the course of years, a large number of the exiles had returned to their old haunts in Nova Scotia.

It must not be forgotten, that thousands of the Acadian French had left the Province, before the expulsion, at the instigation of their French-Canadian brethren, and had seen their dwellings burned by the Indians. Governor Lawrence estimated the number of these self-exiled Acadians, living just north of the Isthmus, as fourteen hundred men capable of bearing arms. These, at once, united with the Indians in taking active measures against the English. A schooner, carrying six guns, on her way to Annapolis Royal, laden with provisions for the garrison, with an artillery officer as passenger, was captured by the Indians while at anchor in Passamequoddy Bay. It was affirmed, that five hundred French were lurking about the woods in Nova Scotia, and that an attack on Annapolis, in the spring of 1756, was projected by French and Indians, but no such action was taken.

The year 1758, which saw the overthrow of French power in Cape Breton, is famous for the formation of an Elective

Assembly in Nova Scotia. As the highest English authority had declared, that the ordinances of the Council at Halifax had not the force of Provincial laws, such a step was considered necessary. The New England people were hesitating about settling in the Province, until better guarantee of a legal status was assured. In 1759, the Province was divided into five counties—Annapolis, Kings, Cumberland, Lunenburg and Halifax—each sending two members to the Assembly, while Annapolis and other towns sent two each. On the meeting of the new Assembly, in 1761, Annapolis County was represented by Joseph Woodmass and John Steele, the town by Joseph Winniett and Thomas Day. After the establishment of representative institutions, the people of New England informed the Governor that they were ready to occupy the lands vacated by the Acadians. The Government quickly agreed to bring settlers free of expense, and grant certain concessions and privileges. The lands abandoned by the French had lain vacant for four years. The dykes, which required constant attention, had fallen into disrepair, admitting the salt water in many places, to the temporary ruin of the crops. The numerous animals had been taken to the German settlements, appropriated by the authorities or perished during the rigors of winter, and the tenements that remained were demanding repairs to prevent them falling into decay. The occupation of these lands was necessary to their preservation.

In June, 1759, the draft of a grant of Granville township was approved, conferring rights on Mr. Crocker, Mr. Grant, and one hundred and thirty-eight others. A grant of land in Annapolis was made to Messrs. Felch, Evans, Bent, and others, to the number of one hundred and twelve. One hundred acres were to be allowed each settler, and fifty acres to every member of his family, on condition that the land be cultivated in thirty years. For the encouragement of the immigrants, every township containing fifty families was to be entitled to send two representatives to the General Assembly. In May, 1760, forty families had arrived at Annapolis, and begun the restoration of that beautiful valley, which is now euphemistically spoken of as the Garden of Nova Scotia. In the year 1763, the districts of Annapolis and Granville contained one hundred and ten families, with fifty-five hundred acres of cleared land. These families, with the other English-speaking immigrants, were all from the New England provinces, so soon to be in revolt against the Mother Country.

As we have pointed out, a few Acadians succeeded in eluding the soldiery in 1755, others returned secretly to the province, until we find ninety of them about Annapolis in 1762. But under what changed conditions did they come. They were no longer the occupants of comfortable abodes, the lords of their own broad acres. An alien race, speaking another language, was possessor of these grand intervales, and their former owners were the hired labourers who toiled as menials, where once they reigned supreme. In July, 1762, one hundred and thirty French from Annapolis and Kings, were taken to Halifax, under escort of militia, to work upon the fortifications. At the close of the war, in 1763, more were encouraged to return. In 1772, we find the Government, giving lands in the township of Clare, to Acadians who had taken the oath of allegiance, an act that gives evidence of the willingness of the authorities to deal towards them with forbearance. Nor has either party ever had occasion to regret the adoption of a more conciliatory attitude. These repatriated Acadians have, ever since, been the most law-abiding citizens of our country, conspicuous among a diligent people for their simple faith and tireless industry.

At this period, we have few records of events connected with Annapolis. The year, 1765, began an agitation that did not cease, till the American Colonies had finally separated from Great Britain. But five years had elapsed, since these very people had come by thousands into the province to occupy the Acadian lands. We may correctly gauge the outflow of their sympathy towards their revolting relatives, though, with few exceptions, they accepted their position as citizens of a new country, which they were bound to defend from attack. The troops in Nova Scotia were hastily removed to strengthen the hands of the Colonial Governors. In 1768, the soldiers at Annapolis and other outposts were withdrawn for concentration in Halifax, a small guard alone remaining to protect the ordnance and stores.

Thus swiftly are new situations created in the intercourse of peoples. Those who had for half a century stood as sponsors and strong guardians of the weakling province, and had peopled it with their best blood, were compelled by the strong tide of affairs to see it pass forever from their connection.

CHAPTER XI.

AMERICAN REVOLUTION—FRENCH WAR—WAR OF 1812—ROADS—
REPRESENTATIVES—CHURCHES—SCHOOLS—SOCIETIES—CHURCH-
YARD.

1775-1897.

The last chapter of this eventful story lies before us. We have seen the hardy Norman, Breton and Poictevan striving to maintain the honour of sunny France, against repeated assaults of the resolute New Englander. Again, we have followed the varying fortunes of these New England men, in their dauntless endeavour to withstand the tides of hostile invasion that surged in repeated billows against their defences. Throughout the periods of French and British rule down to the conquest of Canada, in 1760, there had been no security to life or property in Annapolis Royal. When the French retired from Canada, in agreement with the terms of the Treaty of Paris, the wearied inhabitants might well have said, "the day of peace and progress has dawned at last"; but, in the irony of fate, the period of distraction and unrest was still to be extended.

The new danger to be apprehended, arose from neither lurking savage nor envious Frenchman, but from their brothers of the British colonies, who wished to unite the Nova Scotian with themselves in their struggle against the Mother Country. Embittered at its refusal to take up arms against Great Britain, the revolting colonies attempted hostile movements against the Province. The newly arrived settlers in the Annapolis Valley brought no grievance with them. They came into possession of a magnificent heritage at the hands of the British Government, and self interest bade them remain true to British connection, even at the cost of severing personal and kindred ties. When the regulars were withdrawn from Annapolis, in 1768, these colonial residents were enrolled as a militia to protect the place against attack of rebel privateers, and most of them took the oath of allegiance and fidelity to the King. The New England people, at the outbreak of war, had fortified Machias, and having made a successful attack against Fort Frederick, on the St. John, were planning an aggressive movement on the fort at Annapolis, and gathering information about the disposition of its people. In the year 1775, a number of cannon were sent from Halifax to replace guns that had become unfit for use. In the same year, Governor Legge asks the Home Government to grant funds towards putting the roads into better condition, to expedite transport of troops, and states that the fort at Annapolis should be repaired and garrisoned with four companies of regulars. A sloop of war was stationed in the Bay of Fundy, between Annapolis and the St. John, in 1776.

The years that followed were fraught with anxiety to the farmers of the valley and the fishermen along the shores. Reports were rife of armed craft preparing to make a descent upon the Nova Scotia villages, and many captures were made by privateers on both sides. Annapolis, so often threatened, was not permitted to escape altogether. On the night of August twenty-eighth, 1781, two American privateers, mounting twenty-two guns, and carrying large crews, entered the Basin and reached the town before the break of day. The sentries at the block-house and sally-port were seized before they could give an alarm, and the small garrison of militia were surprised while asleep in barracks, and all made prisoners. In the early dawn, the enemy surrounded the principal houses of the town, and having roused the inmates, marched the men and boys to the block-house or ditch of the fort, where they were left under guard. The privateersmen then proceeded to plunder every house and store of what goods, furniture, clothing, plate, even wearing apparel, they could lay their hands on. After spiking the cannon, they sailed away on the falling tide, leaving the townsmen of Annapolis Royal to enjoy, as best they could, under such conditions, the sweets of liberty. In May, 1782, the townspeople were in a state of alarm, for several days, at the presence of an American sloop of war in the Basin, but their fears were allayed when a British armed sloop entered and captured the intruder.

At this time, Loyalists were coming to Annapolis from the theatre of war in America. There arrived in the month of October, nearly twenty ships bringing one thousand people. A month later fifteen hundred came in from New York. For six months they continued to come, until nearly six thousand of these hapless people, worn with disease and privation, were gathered in the vicinity of Annapolis Royal. Rents were exorbitantly high, and the necessaries of life scarce and dear. Every dwelling in the town was crowded. Hundreds were accommodated in the church ; but crowds of unfortunates, many of whom were persons of education and refinement, had no shelter whatever. Their condition was deplorable, until measures were completed to remove them to less congested quarters. As the military occupied so much land in the very heart of the town, the Loyalists were not able to obtain homesteads in Annapolis Royal. Many of them removed at once to other localities, but a few remained in the neighbourhood for a number of years, partially dependent on the bounty of the British Government. In January, 1787, Amos Botsford, agent for the Loyalists, writes from Annapolis, praising the soil and situation. He says, " Some of our people have chosen Conway, Digby. Others give the preference to St. John. We are settled here for the winter ; some at the fort, some in the town, and others extended up the Annapolis

River nearly twenty miles." The peace of 1783 was hailed with joy by the people of this valley, who had lived for years a life of constant apprehension. Nor were all their troubles over when the war ended. The lawless spirits who found a field for exercise on board the numerous privateers, in time of war, were sometimes a source of danger on the conclusion of peace. Fifty such desperadoes formed a plot to pillage the town of Annapolis, on the night of the anniversary of the Queen's Birthday, 1785. They were to make an attack when the principal citizens were engaged at an anniversary ball, loot the houses and stores, kill any one who offered resistance, place their plunder on board vessel, and make their escape to the United States. The arrest and imprisonment of the ringleader disarranged these plans.

In 1786, the mail service between Annapolis and Halifax was inaugurated, by the employment of a carrier to take letters once a fortnight during the summer, to be withdrawn, one infers, like "The Flying Bluenose," during the winter. On the declaration of war against France, in 1793, Governor Wentworth took active measures to enroll and equip the militia of the province. There were in Annapolis County two military organizations; one of militia, under command of Colonel Milledge, and another, forming a portion of the King's Nova Scotia regiment, raised that year and commanded by Colonel Barclay of Annapolis, subsequently by Colonel Bayard. A body of Acadians was under arms as well, to give testimony in deeds that their allegiance was genuine. Colonel Barclay, who represented Annapolis in the Assembly, and was for a time speaker, made urgent representations to Governor Wentworth respecting repairs upon the fort at Annapolis. A large French fleet at this time gathered in the Chesapeake, whose presence in American waters aroused serious apprehensions. On alarming news reaching Halifax of the approach of the hostile armament, a call was made upon the country militia for assistance. Over one thousand men promptly responded. Of this force Governor Wentworth proudly writes : "Perhaps a finer body of athletic, healthy young men were never assembled in any country, nor men more determined to do their duty." The Granville company, under Captain Willet, made the march of one hundred and thirty-five miles in thirty-five hours, and gave occasion to the spirited lines by Mrs. Irene Elder Morton, which we have with the author's permission inserted. The fleet did not make the apprehended attack upon the city, and the militia returned to their homes at the end of a month. As French privateers were doing great damage to colonial trade and even threatening the coast settlements, we find the authorities at Halifax forwarding guns and ammunition to Annapolis in 1794, with orders to the commissary in charge to place the water front of the fort in a state of good repair to withstand any possible attack.

In the year 1794, society in Annapolis Royal was stirred by a visit from H.R.H. Prince Edward, who afterwards became Duke of Kent and father of our Queen. His stay of six weeks was the occasion of much entertainment, the gossip of which is to-day a tradition among the town-folk.

At the beginning of the short peace between England and France, in 1802, the Nova Scotia regiment was disbanded, Colonel Bayard retiring on half-pay. The respite, however, was short. On the renewal of war in 1804, Nova Scotia shared in common with other colonies the dread of naval attack, until the news of Trafalgar completely dispelled such apprehensions. But, no sooner was one cause of disquietude removed than another took its place. In 1807, the Governor was informed that war was likely to arise between the United States and Great Britain, and that an Irishman named Emmet was proposing to raise a force to conquer Nova Scotia. Steps were at once taken to strengthen the defences at all points exposed to attack; two thousand men were armed for special service in the province, two hundred of whom were quartered in Annapolis Royal. The military spirit was in the ascendant in the ancient capital, and the eyes of the more militant town people were gladdened at the sight of British regiments on the march to strengthen the forces in the sister province; for communication with St. John was carried on by way of Annapolis.

The wrathful mutterings culminated in actual conflict between Great Britain and the United States, in 1812. Nova Scotia suffered no hostile invasion, but the visits of the troublesome privateers were constantly apprehended. In August, 1812, the captain of one of these craft, with one of his officers, was captured while on shore near Digby, and lodged in the dungeon at Annapolis for safe keeping. The country around was in a state of alarm, anticipating attack at any time. Our life in this nineteenth century is so peaceful and undisturbed, that we are scarcely able to appreciate the strain and tension of nerve under such conditions as then prevailed. An incident of that year may raise a smile, even while we sympathize with the nervous terror of a people wrought to panic pitch. One afternoon, the boom of a cannon from the fort caught the ears of the distraught inhabitants. As far as that sound reached, every man stopped his work and awaited with anxiety what was to follow. They were not long kept in suspense; again, came borne on the wind the deep boom of the discharge, and again, it was repeated. One gun, followed by two, was the signal agreed upon, to summon the militia for the defence of the fort. Men seized muskets, powder-horns and bullets, gathered provisions for three days' absence, and hastened forward to repel the invader. As they approached the town, they met terror-stricken women and children, with their valuables in bundles, fleeing to a place of safety. The fort was fully manned, the martial leader ready for the attack, which the enemy hesitated to begin, for the good and sufficient reason that the half dozen plaster-laden craft seeking shelter in the commodious waters of the Basin, had no hostile intentions whatever; and their skippers were greatly surprised that a few English schooners should be mistaken for a fleet· of Yankee privateers. The next year, 1813, a force of regulars was sent to relieve the militiamen in part of their onerous duties. There is in the possession of Mr. Roach, in the town, the order-book used by his father, Lieutenant James Roach, on duty as Quarter-Master among the embodied militia, in 1814. The names of many men on the roster are familiar in Annapolis to-day. Lieutenant-Colonels Darling, Herbert, and Winniett held office on the regular and militia lists. Robert Duport was Commissary General. We read that a party of eighteen American prisoners started the march for Halifax on April twenty-fifth, under a guard of garrison militia as far as " Leonards "—Paradise—where the escort were to be relieved by a detachment from that district. During this war, provisions were at times very scarce among the good people of the town, whose purses could illy spare five guineas for a barrel of flour. The close of the war, in 1814, brought to an end the incessant fears of the inhabitants, now utterly tired of the ceaseless unrest, and desirous to bend their energies to the worthy task of developing the great resources of their country. Our record has been one of war and strife : the smoke of battle hangs like a sable pall over the changing story. As a glad harbinger of brighter days, we read that the first quarter of the nineteenth century saw a light-house placed at Digby Passage. The fitful flash of death-dealing cannon had often blazed, to forbid approach by that pathway of the sea ; in happy contrast, this beacon was to throw its radiance afar, to invite with cheery welcome the wide world's argosies.

At this time there were two roads open between Annapolis and Halifax. One, the great western post road, was first built between the French settlements of Port Royal and Grand Pré, then extended to Pizequid, Windsor, and continued to the new City of Halifax immediately on Governor Cornwallis' arrival, as he depended upon the French settlers on the Avon and Canard for his supplies. This road crossed the Avon River six miles above the Town of Windsor, until the completion of the covered bridge opposite the town. The bridge across the Annapolis at Bridgetown was built in 1803. In 1816, a stage coach made two trips per week over this road between Windsor and Halifax—fare for round trip, twelve dollars. In 1815, a new road to Halifax was surveyed, much shorter than the Windsor road. This was called the military road, on account of its being settled by soldiers who came to America after the peace that followed Waterloo. La Rose, Dalhousie, Sherbrooke, are on this road, which reaches Halifax across Hammond's Plains. Other roads in the vicinity of Annapolis Royal give evidence of military origin. Their very names, have a martial flavour. The Waldeck Line, the Hessian Line are districts bordering Annapolis Basin on the south, settled in the year 1784, by loyal emigrants and soldiers of the German legion, who had received their discharge at the close of the Revolutionary War. The road leading to Liverpool was begun in 1804. As a healthful sign of increasing intercourse and public spirit, as well as an indication of improvement in the roads of the province, we note the establishment of a tri-weekly stage between Halifax and Annapolis in the year 1828, for which service three hundred dollars per year were voted by the Assembly. One hundred and fifty dollars were given the same year for steam service between Annapolis and St. John. The coach to Halifax, which was after a time changed to a daily, continued to be the popular means of travel until the opening of the Windsor and Annapolis Railway in 1869. The town assumed a somewhat different appearance at that time, as about thirty dwellings were torn down or removed to make place for the railway grounds. The continuation of the railway line to Digby, across the difficult waters of the Moose and Bear rivers, involving the withdrawal of the Saint John steamer from Annapolis, are matters of recent interest. The cessation of steamboat trips is especially deplored by the tourist, who is thereby deprived of one of the most delightful experiences in Nova Scotia travel—a trip on the charming waters of Annapolis Basin. The limits of the present effort forbid mention of even important matters of recent occurrence.

In the earlier days of the century, the town presented the appearance of an aristocratic, and conservative community. The leading residents were descendants of former provincial officials, either military or civil, and occupied a high place in provincial society. The presence of the garrison lent its influence to enhance the gaiety of social existence. There were always a few great houses whose doors were open in a generous and profuse hospitality, that must have been deeply enjoyable to the stranger, in that day of public discomfort. Among those who were transient or permanent residents are names that have been renowned in our country's annals. Sir Colin Campbell—Lord Clyde—as a young man, was an officer in this garrison ; Sir Fenwick Williams, the defender of Kars and subsequently Lieutenant-Governor of Nova Scotia, was born and passed his boyhood here ; Thomas Chandler Haliburton, "one of the most eminent literary men British America ever produced," lived in Annapolis, practised at the bar, and represented the county in the Assembly ; Thomas Ritchie, Judge of the Supreme Court, had his home at "The Grange," in the midst of a broad domain. The men who successively represented the town in the Provincial Assembly were Jonathan Hoar, Joseph Winniett, Thomas Day, O.

8

Wheelock, Phineas Lovett, Colonel Delaney, Thomas Barclay, Thomas Walker, John Harris, Thomas Ritchie, John Robertson, James Lovett, Elnathan Whitman, Henry Gates, Alfred Whitman, Moses Shaw. Township representation ceased in the year 1859, in which year Annapolis, as a County, sent three members.

Of the five churches in the town, the Baptist and Presbyterian are of comparatively late organization. The former body built a place of worship in 1874, and called Rev. T. A. Higgins, of Wolfville, to the pastorate. Before that date, services were held in the house of Mr. Freeman Barteaux, and in the Court House. The Presbyterian church was built in 1859, when Rev. G. A. Murray was pastor. Missionaries of that faith had previously preached in Temperance Hall, near the slip. On a stone in the Roman Catholic cemetery, we read that Anthony Hannon built the church near by, in the year 1835. Before that time, that body worshipped at the house of Michael Mehan, which stood nearly opposite the store of Messrs. Pickels & Mills. Mention of the early structures built by the French has been made in the introduction. The first Methodist church was erected in Annapolis, about the year 1799. It stood on the corner of Church and St. Anthony streets, where it may still be seen, though devoted to other than clerical uses. In 1846, the present edifice was built at the head of Ferry Slip, and moved to its present location in 1867. The history of Methodism in Annapolis Royal goes back as far as the year 1782, when William Black, an itinerant, visited the town. In 1786, nearly one hundred members were reported on mission roll from Digby, Annapolis and Granville, at which time efforts were being made to build a church. The body grew under the labours of successive missionaries, until in 1831, we find a resident minister in Annapolis town, and a church building at Granville Ferry.

We are indebted to Rev. H. D. DeBlois, rural dean, for the fullest information respecting the Church of England. He thinks that the first building used for the Church of England service was the French parish church of St. Ann, situated near the present freight station of the Dominion and Atlantic Railway. It is described as "a building two stories high, which looked more like a barn than a house of God." During the incumbency of the Rev. Jacob Bailey, in 1784, either a new building, sixty feet by forty, and capable of seating five hundred people, was built, or the old house was remodeled, and a bell tower with a bell added. The old name of St. Ann was dropped at that time, and that of St. Luke adopted. In 1815, the present parish church of St. Luke was erected on land given by the British Government, which also contributed five hundred pounds sterling, on condition that a portion of the building was reserved for the use of the soldiers of the garrison. The first Protestant service in Nova Scotia, of which we have record, was held in the garrison on October tenth, 1710, when divine service was conducted by Rev. John Harrison, the newly appointed chaplain. Mr. Harrison became a member of the first council appointed by Governor Phillips, and was living in Annapolis as late as 1728. Rev. Richard Watts probably succeeded him about 1730. A prominent divine of the early days was Rev. Thomas Wood, who was connected with the parish from 1753 to 1778. He was instrumental in obtaining grants of land for church purposes, and in building churches throughout the county. "His remains lie interred at Annapolis in an unmarked and unknown grave." Another pioneer labourer was Rev. Jacob Bailey, who came to Nova Scotia as a Loyalist refugee, and assumed charge of the Annapolis church in 1782. The suffering Loyalists who arrived at Annapolis received great kindness at his hands. He died in 1808. Rev. Edwin Gilpin, who died in 1860, was the last minister to perform the duties of garrison chaplain, as the troops were withdrawn during his rectorship.

Annapolis Royal is the seat of the County Academy, which draws an annual sum of five hundred dollars from the Provincial Government. The school grounds are said to be the finest in the province, and we hope may some early day grace a building equally the pride of the town. The former school house stood in the "White House Field," near the Presbyterian church. In the records of the " Society for the Propagation of the Gospel," year 1729, we read that Rev. Richard Watts, about to go, in 1727, as chaplain to Annapolis, asked the Society for an allowance for teaching the poor children there. They gave him ten pounds a year, and doubled the sum in 1731. He opened his school in Annapolis at Easter, 1728, with fifty children under his instruction. He built, at his own cost, a " school house for the good of the publick, and especially for the poorer sort," and appointed it for that use forever. This building stood near the present railway station, and passed, after a time, into the hands of a master who refused to surrender possession until it was beyond repair. This record is interesting, as affording the first mention of secular instruction in Nova Scotia, that is, by the British ; for D'Aunay is said to have established schools here in the early French period. In 1811, an act was passed by the Provincial Assembly to establish a Grammar School in Annapolis, for which one hundred pounds per annum were granted, with an additional fifty pounds, when there were more than thirty pupils. In 1826, this sum was increased to two hundred pounds yearly. Haliburton in his " History of Nova Scotia," informs us that the Academy, previously mentioned as standing near the Presbyterian church, was built in the year 1827, partly by voluntary subscription, and partly by Provincial aid. " It receives for its support an annual vote of two hundred pounds, which, together with the tuition money, enables the

trustees to engage two masters to take charge of the institution. The building contains two distinct schools, one of
which is devoted to classical education, and the other to the
elementary and higher branches that are commonly taught in
English schools."

The town does not suffer for lack of societies, in the names
of which it is intensely loyal to local prestige ; for Annapolis
Royal Lodge A.F. & A.M., Port Royal Lodge of Good
Templars, and Tawopskik Encampment I.O.O.F., represent,
severally, English, French and Indian periods in our varied
history. Western Star Lodge I.O.O.F., was established in
1874, and has ever since enjoyed a vigorous existence. In
1893, Tawopskik Encampment was organized, mainly through
the efforts of " Joe Edwards," for many years the popular
conductor on the Dominion and Atlantic Railway, and known
far and wide to the travelling public. The Masonic Order is
represented by Eureka Chapter, Royal Arch Masons, and
Annapolis Royal Lodge, Master Masons. Annapolis is a
centre of interest to all Brethren of the Mystic Tie, for
Masonry is here venerable with age. On the shores of this
Basin was found the earliest evidence of Freemasonry on the
Continent of North America. In the year 1827, Dr. Charles
Jackson, the celebrated American geologist, discovered on the
shore, at Goat Island, a stone bearing the Masonic emblems,
the square and compass, together with the figures 1606. This
stone is supposed by our best informed antiquarians, to mark
some important transaction, probably the first sowing of seed
by Poutrincourt, in August of that year. The Masonic
inscription indicates under what auspices this stone was
erected. It came into the hands of the Canadian Institute,
and has recently been placed in the walls of their new building in Toronto, inscription inside, well covered with mortar, to
preserve its secret from the prying eyes of the curious vulgar.
The following is from the minutes of the Grand Lodge of

Massachusetts, whose archives contain the earliest Masonic records now known to be in existence on the continent: "Aside from the fact that it affords of the earliest footprints of Masonry in North America, the locality (Annapolis) has other claims upon the attention of the fraternity. It is known that Sir William Alexander, jr., who was left in command of the Scotch fort at Granville in 1628, was made a Fellowcraft in Edinburgh Lodge, Scotland, in 1634. It is assumed as not improbable, that he was initiated an Entered Apprentice by some of the brethren, whom he found at Port Royal," during his sojourn in Nova Scotia, as no record of initiation is found in Scotland. "Our Society may well unite with the historian in the opinion, that there are few localities in America around which the memories of the shadowy past more interestingly cling, than around the ancient town of Annapolis, where the Masonic fire has burned with singular persistency." In 1733, the Provincial Grand Lodge of Massachusetts was organized in Boston. In 1734, a deputation was sent from Boston to organize a lodge in Philadelphia, of which Benjamin Franklyn was first Master. In 1738, the R. W. Grand Master in Boston granted a deputation, "at ye petition of Sundry Brethren at Annapolis, in Nova Scotia," to hold a lodge there, and appointed Major Erasmus James Phillips, D.G.M. In the minutes of Grand Lodge of Massachusetts for year 1741, we note that Brethren E. Phillips and Sheriff were present from Annapolis.. We thus find the appearance of Freemasonry in Annapolis, under the British *regime*, to be contemporaneous with its establishment in Boston and Philadelphia, the first cities on the continent, and may look with pride at the *strength* and *establishment* of an institution whose foundations are sunk in the matrix of the years. Unfortunately, the records of the fraternity in the town were burned in a disastrous fire a few years ago, when the Masonic hall was consumed with valuable regalia and jewels. Annapolis Royal

Lodge is a flourishing representative of the Ancient Order, holding a charter from the Grand Lodge of Nova Scotia since 1863, having been before that No. 1047, on the roll of the Grand Lodge of England. The erection of a spacious hall in the Victorian Jubilee year, 1897, marks a new departure in its honourable history.

Before taking our leave of the town, let us enter the gateway of the old English burial ground, where great and small mingle their common dust. Its grassy mounds, as well, are slowly sinking to a common level, and confirming with sad emphasis the truth of the statement, so abhorrent to our sensibilities, that we find our graves in the memories of our friends. A few of the lots in this ground are cared for, but, for the most part, little attention is bestowed upon the graves. If we are not relatives of those who slumber there, we are at least citizens of a town that owes itself a duty to preserve from destruction the precious mementos of its memorable past. The public spirit of our citizens, amply evident in many enterprises, will ere long compel attention to this historic, but too little cherished, churchyard. We wander through its winding paths, searching the records now scarcely decipherable on the moss-covered head-stones. 1720—1740, mark the dates on stones erected to the memory of wives of Samuel Douglas, a garrison official. Head-stones were difficult to be obtained in the early days, and many an eminent and worthy citizen lies in an unmarked grave ; 1727, Margaret Winniett, five years of age—the only mention of a family name that stood foremost in the annals of the town ; 1788, Thomas Williams, Commissary ; 1806, Thomas Williams, Commissary — the father and grandfather of Sir Fenwick Williams ; 1818, Dr. Hinkle, Staff-Surgeon, long a leading citizen in the old town ; 1812, Amelia, daughter of Phineas and Margaret Lovett— Ph. Lovett represented the town in the Provincial Assembly in 1800; 1843 is the date affixed to a stone marking the graves of two soldiers who were drowned in the swift waters of the river, which has claimed many a victim since the unfortunate D'Aunay sank beneath its surface. Many officers of the garrison here found a resting-place among the people they defended. Thrust from its position by the growth of a vigorous thorn tree, there lies a stone with the following inscription : "In memory of Gregoria Remonia Antonia, wife of James Norman . . . died 1862, aged 72 years—a native of Spain." She rests far from the vineyards and orange groves of Andalusia, where once her youthful beauty commanded homage. It is said she accompanied her husband on the battle-field at Waterloo, and witnessed the tremendous struggle of that eventful day. Families lie buried here whose honoured names are of more than provincial reputation, sleeping calmly beside the humble poor whose lowly resting-place is destitute of "storied urn or animated bust." The stranger will remark a deep excavation extending across the ground. If he makes examination, he will find the mound formed by the earth thrown up from this trench to be covered with graves, some of whose head-stones bear the date 1812. It will thus be seen that the trench is very old, and probably was dug by Nicholson's men, in 1710, when, in besieging the fort, they are said to have constructed a battery within one hundred yards of the parapet.

We pass from the burial ground into the inclosure of old Fort Anne. We view with keen sense of appreciation the extensive repairs that are being effected upon its dilapidated buildings, which will soon again resume their former substantial appearance. But when all shall have been done, who among us can in imagination restore the appearance which the neat and well gravelled square presented, when the cross of St. George floated from the flag-staff ? When, beside the mounted gun, the pyramid of shot gave evidence of earnest deeds ? When the tireless sentinel paced his steady beat, by day and night, silent, save for his challenge to an intruder? When the shrill clarion of the bugle-call rang its echoes, and the thunderous discharge of artillery rolled in repeated reverberations among our hills? When the brilliant uniforms of officers and the flashing brightness of military equipment afforded a gaudy pageant to the delighted populace; doubly delighted, if the soldiery chanced to be the lads of "Bonnie Scotland" swinging proudly by in kilt and tartan to the martial strains of the inspiring pibroch? Memory enables our elders to recall such scenes as were here witnessed, before the last soldier marched out at the garrison gate, and closed the record of noble and distinguished service in Annapolis Royal. The young among us in this day of swift rivalry, though not taught to foster a military spirit, stand in urgent need of the best qualities of mind and heart, to win an honourable place in the ranks of their compeers. They should gather inspiration from the story of the past, and, while enjoying in peace and quiet a precious heritage, let them not forget to emulate the noble achievements of those by whom that heritage was won.

THE TRAMP OF THE BOYS FROM GRANVILLE.*

A SONG BY MRS. IRENE ELDER MORTON.

Just one hundred years ago,—did I write in ninety-three—
Came a warning to New Scotia's capital,
    That the lilies of old France
    Crowned war-ships on the advance,
To retake the land she once had loved so well.

    Then the sturdy men, who kept
    Watch for country and for king,
Trained the guns, and wheeled the cannon into line ;
    And the citadel shone true,
    In the red, the white, and blue,
Where St. George and the Union Jack entwine.

    Then they gave a swift command ;
    " Sound the bugle through the land,"
And in answer to it came a thousand men,
    From the east, the west, the north,
    In fair columns they pour forth,
Quick to rally round the flag that made them free.

    But the swiftest on the road—
    With a double-quick they strode,—
Was the gallant, gallant Granville company.
    Then Hurrah ! Hurrah ! Hurrah !
    For the boys from Granville.
Hurrah ! Hurrah for the tramp of the boys from Granville.

    'Tis a little late to cheer ;
    For they've slumbered many a year,
In their graves, where the bravest rest at last ;
    But their dust shall honoured be,
    And their names, we yet may see,
Hunted up from some old record of the past.
    Then Hurrah ! Hurrah ! Hurrah !
    For the boys from Granville.
Hurrah ! Hurrah for the tramp of the boys from Granville.

Now, just tell our lady Queen,
That, by this song, we mean
To tell her, that in any future day,
Should her enemies appear,
We shall strive to make it clear,
Who will do the better work in the fray.

For Canadian boys are true
To the British white and blue,
And the colonies are jewels of the crown ;
We will stand by home and Queen,
And no power shall come between,
And no hand shall pull the Royal Standard down.

---

* Intelligence being received at Halifax, in 1793, that a French fleet was at New York, preparing to leave for the north, a council of war was held and it was decided that the militia should be called from the principal outposts. A thousand men responded in a short time, one company under Captain Willet, marching from Granville, a distance of one hundred and thirty-five miles, in thirty-five hours, and that over a road scarcely deserving the name.

INDEX.

A.

Acadia, called La Cadie, 13.
Latour in, 31.
La Borgne comes to, 37.
French asking for, 38.
French regain possession of, 38.
Acadians, near Port Royal, 65.
invited to settle in Cape Breton, 70.
refuse to take oath of allegiance, 70.
finally take oath, 71.
justice and constable chosen from, 73.
trade with Louisburg, 75.
refuse to trade with English, 85.
influence of fight at Grand Pré, 88.
increase of, 91.
expulsion of, 94-97.
return to Nova Scotia, 99.
sent to Halifax, 99.
lands in Clare given to, 99.
enrolled in militia, 104.
Adams, John, 73.
Aix La Chapelle, treaty of, 89.
Allen's Creek, 32.
Alexander, Sir William, 25.
forms company to trade in Nova Scotia, 25.
writes to Captain Forester, 28.
Annapolis Basin, 1-3.
Annapolis Royal, 3.
proclaimed, 65.
trade elsewhere in Nova Scotia forbidden, 66.
invested by Indians, 68.
soldiers arrive at, 69.

Annapolis Royal, English families at, 74
trade with Boston, 76.
stores sent to, 77.
exposed state of settlement, 79.
attacked by Du Vivier, 81.
attacked by Maran, 84.
Ramesay arrives at, 87.
as capital, 92.
New England settlers, 98.
captured by American privateers, 102.
Loyalists come to, 103.
plot to plunder, 104.
false alarm in, 106.
churches in, 110.
societies in, 113.
Annapolis Royal Lodge, 113.
Annapolis County, 98.
Anne, fort, description of, 5-7.
Anson, Admiral, victory of, 89.
Appleton, Colonel, 50.
Armstrong, Lieut.-Gov., 71.
servant punished, 74.
Arsenault Pierre, 39.
settles Chignecto, 39.
Assembly, Elective, formed, 98.
Annapolis representatives, 109.
Attacks on Port Royal, 6.
Austrian Succession, war of, 78.

B.

Barclay, Colonel, 104.
Baronets of Nova Scotia formed, 25.
Bayard, Colonel, 104.
Bear River, 3.

ACADIA UNIVERSITY

HORTON ACADEMY ✦ ✦ ACADIA SEMINARY

GEO. E. CORBITT

ANNAPOLIS ROYAL, NOVA SCOTIA

Dealer in

Staple and Fancy
Groceries XXX

Also

HARD AND SOFT COAL

It is the place to buy right, as he imports all his goods direct from manufacturers and sells at City Prices

---

Edwin L. Fisher

MERCHANT TAILOR

Importer of Foreign and Domestic Woollens

The lowest priced Custom Tailoring Establishment in the Province.

SATISFACTION GUARANTEED

STORES:
ANNAPOLIS ROYAL and BRIDGETOWN, N.S.

Complete Stock at both Stores

H. E. GILLIS   FRED. W. HARRIS

GILLIS & HARRIS

Barristers,
Solicitors,
Notaries Public,
Etc.

ANNAPOLIS ROYAL, N.S.

R. S. MILLER

MANUFACTURER AND DEALER IN

 All kinds of Light and Heavy Harness, Horse Furnishings, Whips, Rugs, Brushes, Oils, Etc.

ANNAPOLIS ROYAL, N.S.

30662631R00084